Dear Friend,

The year 1997 marks the 20th anniversary of Larox. It is a wonderful milestone for us, and we are pleased with the progress we have made. We know, however, that our accomplishments are not simply the result of innovations or hard-working employees. We have grown and prospered thanks to our partners and customers, whose interests we put first. As a symbol of this, we have decided to send you something that addresses the most universal of interests: food.

The publication you hold chronicles the beauty of Finland's culture, traditions and gastronomy. After all, international business is a bridge between countries and peoples, and we believe that sharing cultures and traditions is an important part of the bridge-building process.

Although the book offers a comprehensive selection of recipes, we felt it appropriate to add one special recipe of our own.

6 Steps to the World's Driest Cake

1. *Combine your favorite cake mix with some water.*
2. *Take a tightly woven cloth and place it over the cake mixture. Apply pressure.*
3. *To achieve the highest cake quality, spread some water evenly over the cake.*
4. *Reapply more pressure, squeezing out every bit of excess liquid.*
5. *Blow compressed air over the cake layer to achieve the desired cake dryness.*
6. *The cake will be so dry at this point that it will automatically eject from the pan.*

Note: conventional ovens are unnecessary

We are pleased to provide you this simple cake recipe. We hope you enjoy it.

Timo Vartiainen
President, Larox Group

LAROX

Separates the best from the rest

Finland-Nature's table

Publisher: Crea Video Oy

Printed in Esan Kirjapaino Oy, Lahti, Finland
Paper Galerie Art silk 170g/m^2 , Metsä Serla Oy / Äänekoski Art Paper Mill, Finland
ISBN 952-9750-10-2

Author: Tiia Koskimies
Design and layout: Minna Hietaniemi and Peter Holmén
Gastronomic planning and recipes: Maija Silvennoinen
Food photography design: Mervi Aropaltio
Food photography: Timo Viljakainen, Studio Viljakainen, Helsinki, Finland
Translation: Paul Westlake and Kristiina Ahovuori

Nature photographs: Tiia Koskimies (2, 3:2/3, 4:1/3, 8:4/4, 52-53, 80, 94-95, 98:1/4, 100: 1/4, 133, 136:4/6, 138:4/6, 145, 148, 158, 160),
Markus Varesvuo (121, 140:1,2,4,5 /6, 141), Timo Viljakainen (3:3/3, 4:2/3, 5:3/3, 28, 68-69,84, 107, 149), Jukka Talikka (146), Fennopress (151)
Nature photo agency / Heikki Aalto (29), Lauri Aarnio (130), Markku Alkioniemi (124-125), Kari Auvinen (10), Patrik Bertrand (50),
Blechinberg Kristian (5:1/3), Hannu Eskonen (15), Pentti Hartikainen (129), Hannu Hautala (122,126,136:1/6,140:6/6,142-143),
Tapio K. Heikkilä (8:3/4), Jukka Heikkinen (66-67), Hannu Huovila (131), Hannu Huttu (7), Arto Hämäläinen (9, 118-119), Heikki Ilasaari (6),
Pentti Johansson (8:2/4, 75), Reijo Juurinen (98:4/4, 100:3/4), Ilpo Kojola (3:1/3), Olli Koponen (14), Jarmo Kovanen (78-79), Lassi Kujala (8:1/4),
Jouko Kuosmanen (130), Kimmo Kuure (155), Teljo Laine (96), Matti Laukkanen (4:3/3), Antti Leinonen (123), Juha Leppävuori (39),
Jorma Luhta (12-13, 152), André Maslennikov (138:3/6), Matti Mela (136:3/6, 153), Paavo Merikukka (74:5/5), Jarkko Mäkineva (51, 65, 99),
Pauli Nieminen (74: 1,2,5/5, 144), Timo Nieminen (86-87, 127), Teijo Nikkanen (38), Heikki Nikki (124-125, 154), Markku Nikki (11),
Aarni Nummila (36-37), Pentti Ojala (98:2/4), Jouni Ojutkangas (100:4/4), Risto Ovaskainen (138:3/6), Timo Patomeri (98:3/4, 101, 120),
Risto Pylvänäinen (139), Mikko Pöllänen (128), Ritva Reinilä (147:1/2), Veikko Rissanen (147:2/2), Martti Roininen (100:2/4),
Reijo Salminen (129, 136:6/6), Erkki Santamala (48-49), Matti Silvennoinen (140:3/6), Kari Soveri (136:5/6), Markku Tano (5:2/3, 97, 136:2/6, 150),
Juha Taskinen (64), Matti Torkkomäki (26-27), Matti Valta (74:3/5, 134-135), Hans Viitasola (102), Reijo Wallin (93), Tuomo Ylinärä (138:5/6), Matti
Ylätupa (138:6/6)

We would like to thank Marimekko and Antiikki Erik .

Our thanks are also due to the Nature photo agency for their expert help and cooperation.

Contents

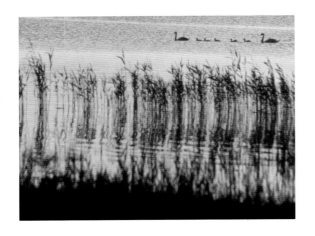

People of the Forest

Finland is forest. It's vital to the Finnish identity. According to research, three out of every four Finns feel that the forest offers very real protection. Many also describe their experience of the forest in much the same way as they recall their earliest childhood experiences of security. The Finnish forest is calming, melodious, gentle and warm. A sanctuary, a place where tranquility reigns.

Until relatively recently, Finnish homesteads were scattered over large areas of forest. This has been instrumental in the conceptualization of Finnishness. Many city dwellers have access to a summer cottage in the middle of a forest or by a lake. At the very least, they dream of it.

After the humdrum of everyday working life, the forest soothes and rejuvenates the soul. It's essential to 'get away from it all', if only for a while. The forest is inspirational. It offers continuity, constantly changing its appearance along with the weather and seasons.

At sunrise, when the dew lingers on spider webs, when bird song is at its most melodious: that's when the forest is at its most beautiful. During those long, hot summer days the forest offers a cooling shade. In the evening and at night the trees give off the warmth of the day, providing a safe and sound slumber land.

Rain invigorates the forest and rarefies the air, making the moss soft underfoot. And when the wind rages the trees howl their age-old stories.

In the spring the forest embodies rebirth.
In the summer it enwraps you
in a thousand greens.
In the autumn it dazzles and exhales.
And in the winter it enraptures your soul.

There's always something new to see and experience in the forest. It also provides the majority of Finns with a living.

Finland's short but brilliant summer enables the forest to supply animals and people with most of their nutritional needs. Our light summer nights produce supreme aromatic berries, herbs and mushrooms.

The wholesome, natural ingredients of our forests do not require complicated cooking methods or strong spices. Finnish food is at its best when prepared plain and simply.

So, join us on a gastronomic tour as we introduce you to *Finland – Nature's table.*

Fish

Every Finn has probably been fishing at some time or other. Finland has nearly two hundred thousand lakes, an abundance of rivers and a long coastline. Summer cottages are located on the sea shore and lake sides. Rowing boats are therefore a useful commodity. In summer evenings Finns spread their nets and go out fishing.

Many fish are caught by private individuals, which may not leave a lot for the little country shops.

Winter's frozen conditions present no problem for fishermen. Nets can be cast underneath the ice. Ice fishing is a very popular, even if a little peculiar, winter pursuit in Finland. Thousands of men and women dress up in extra-warm clothing and go fishing on the ice. A small hole is drilled through the ice by means of an ice drill and the intrepid ice angler just sits there fishing, sometimes for hours. This is yet another opportunity for Finns to fulfill their yearning to be at one with nature. Being able to spend time in a true winter wonderland, alone with one's thoughts, is probably more important than the catch itself.

Nearly one hundred different species of fish swim in Finnish waters. Only about twenty of them, however, end up on the dinner table.

Salmon (Salmo salar) and sea-bred *rainbow trout* (Salmo gairdneri) are the most popular fish for Finns. For the most part, salmon is still eaten in the traditional way; slightly salted. Fresh rainbow trout is on offer practically every day of the year. It's inexpensive and easy to prepare. Salmon is caught in the Baltic Sea with fyke nets. Sport fishermen go fly fishing for large and handsome migratory salmon in the rivers of Lapland.

The most prestigious fish for most Finns, however, is *perch* (Perca fluviatilis). It's also the most endemic, and can be found in most waters except for the petite mountain lakes of Lapland. The flesh of the perch is sweetish and tastes good, grilled, smoked, poached or fried. The largest perch are caught in nets from the sea. Children can catch tiddlers with their rods and weirs.

Pikeperch (Stizostedion lucioperca), related to the perch, is also widely appreciated. Its bones are easily removed and it's frequently favoured by restaurants.

There are many varieties of *whitefish* (Coregonus lavaretus) in Finland. It, too, is popular and can always be found alongside salmon and pikeperch in restaurants. Whitefish is particularly good broiled or smoked. It gives a superbly fresh taste to fish stock. Many fish-eaters prefer slightly-salted whitefish to salmon. Whitefish roe is a real delicacy - Finnish caviar at its best - served on top of blinis, as a filling for baked potatoes or as an ingredient for sauces.

Vendace (Coregonus albula) is considered typically Finnish and the only precious fish professionally caught in shoals. Vendace is best fried in butter. Its roe is small-grained and delicate in taste. In eastern Finland vendace is served as *kukko*, a rye bread crust filled with vendace and slices of pork loin, baked in the oven.

Baltic herring (Clupea harengus membras) has provided the basis for archipelago culture for centuries. It's the most important catch in the Baltic Sea. It's also the cheapest fish to buy. A kilo of Baltic herrings only costs a few marks. More books on Baltic herring have been published in Finland than on any other food. And there are hundreds of ways of preparing it. Traditional Baltic herrings, coated with rye flour and fried in butter, is nevertheless the most popular way of enjoying this versatile fish.

Another scrumptious Finnish fish is *pike* (Esox lucius), often used in fish cakes and loaves. Pike is also a suitable catch for trolling.

Winter is a time for catching *burbot* (Lota lota). Famous for its roe, burbot is ideal for stews and soups.

Flounder (Platichthys flesus) can be categorized as a coastal summer fish. It's particularly delicious when freshly smoked.

Roe Toast

Roe Toast

4 slices white bread
butter
240 g sour cream
150 g whitefish roe
1 small red onion, half sliced and half chopped
fresh dill for garnish
(freshly ground black pepper)

1. Strain the roe in a sieve.
2. Toast the bread and cut into desired shapes.
3. Butter and leave to cool.
4. Whip the sour cream and spoon into a piping bag.
5. Pipe the sour cream onto the sides of the bread slices. Spoon the roe into the middle and decorate with sliced and diced onion and dill.
6. Serve as a starter or a light snack.

Slightly Salted Salmon and Whitefish

Salmon or whitefish, cleaned, scaled and boned
For each 500 g of prepared fish:

1-2 tbsp sea salt
1 tbsp sugar
fresh dill, chopped

1. Divide the fish into two fillets.
2. Lay 1 fillet of fish, skin side down, in a shallow dish. Sprinkle the salt and sugar over the fleshy side. If the fish is to be eaten the following day, use more salt. Add a generous amount of chopped fresh dill.
3. Lay the other fillet on top, skin side up. Sprinkle with more salt.
4. Cover with a plate and a weight. Put in the fridge for at least 24 hours. Turn the fish once.
5. To serve, scrape off the excess salt and cut into thin slices.

Rainbow Trout Roe, Whitefish Roe and Vendace Roe

See picture opposite.

Marinated Baltic Herrings in Mustard Sauce

500 g Baltic herring fillets

Marinade:
500 ml water
100 ml spirit vinegar
1 tbsp coarse sea salt

Sauce:
100 ml sweet mustard
1 tbsp red wine vinegar
2 tsp salt
3 tbsp caster sugar
1/2 tsp finely ground white pepper
100 ml oil
50 ml water
100 ml chopped dill

1. Remove the skin from the Baltic herrings.
2. Mix the marinade ingredients together.
3. Pour the marinade over the fish fillets and allow to marinate for 4 hours.
4. Prepare the sauce. Mix together the mustard, red wine vinegar, salt, sugar and white pepper.
5. Drizzle the oil in, stirring constantly. Dilute the sauce with water. Add the chopped dill.
6. Drain the fish fillets well and place in a dish together with the sauce so that all the fillets are covered in the liquid. Cover with a lid.
7. Leave to marinate for 24 hours. Serve as a starter with boiled potatoes and rye bread.

Slightly Salted Salmon and Pasta Roulade

4 lasagne sheets
water
1 tbsp oil
a pinch of salt

Filling:
100 g plain cream cheese
50 ml single cream
1 tbsp chopped onion
a little chopped garlic
1/2 tbsp lemon juice
freshly ground black pepper
basil
150 g slightly salted or cold-smoked salmon, in slices

Dressing:
200 ml mayonnaise
100 ml crushed tomatoes
1 garlic clove, crushed
2 tbsp chopped parsley
salt and freshly ground black pepper

1. Cook the pasta sheets in a saucepan of boiling water together with the oil and salt, until "al dente".
2. Cool the sheets side-by-side (slightly overlapping each other) on oiled greaseproof paper so that you get one large sheet.
3. Mix the cream with the cream, chopped onions, lemon juice, salt and black pepper.
4. Spread the mixture onto the cool pasta sheets.
5. Sprinkle chopped basil on top.
6. Arrange the salmon slices on top of the mixture side by side and roll the pasta sheet up, like a Swiss roll, using the greaseproof paper to help.
7. Cool in the fridge before slicing. The roulade is at its best the following day.
8. Mix the dressing ingredients together.
9. Cut the roulade into slices and serve with the dressing.

Finnish Fish Soup

3 tbsp butter
1 small onion, chopped
4 medium-sized potatoes, diced
1 litre fish stock
5 whole allspice
a piece of rye bread
500 g boned fillet of fish (perch, pike-perch, salmon, whitefish, Baltic herring), diced
200 ml whipping cream
50 ml chopped dill
salt and freshly ground black pepper

1. Melt the butter in a large saucepan. Sweat the onion and diced potatoes in it.
2. Add the fish stock, allspice and bread.
3. Simmer for about 10 minutes, until the potatoes are almost done.
4. Add the fish cubes and whipping cream. Bring to the boil.
5. Season with salt and pepper. Add the dill just before serving. Serve with toasted, buttered rye bread.

Baltic Herrings Seasoned with Rye Crisp Powder

4 tbsp butter
100 ml chopped onion
200 ml powder, ground from rye crisps
600 g Baltic herring fillets
salt and freshly ground black pepper
50 ml chopped dill
120 g sour cream

1. Sweat the onion in the butter. Add the rye crisp powder and fry briefly. Leave to cool.
2. Spread the fish fillets, skin side down, on a board.
3. Season with salt and pepper.
4. Sprinkle the onion and rye crisp powder mixture onto the fillets.
5. Fold the fish lengthwise and transfer into a greased ovenproof dish.
6. Sprinkle the rest of the powder on top.
7. Season the sour cream with salt, pepper and dill.
8. Pour the mixture onto the fish. Cook in a 200°C oven for about 25 minutes.
9. Serve with boiled or mashed potatoes and pickled beetroot.

Fried Vendace on a Spinach Bed

400 g vendace, scaled and gutted
salt
100 ml rye flour
3 tbsp butter

Spinach bed:
2 tbsp butter
200 g fresh spinach, stems removed
1 small onion, chopped
salt and freshly ground white pepper

To garnish: fresh dill

1. Sprinkle the fish with salt.
2. Mix a pinch of salt with the rye flour. Coat the fish with the mixture.
3. Brown the butter in a frying pan and lay the fish in it. Turn when browned on one side.
4. Prepare the spinach bed. Melt the butter in a pan.
5. Add the onion and spinach leaves. Sweat for 2 minutes and season.
6. Make a bed of spinach onto a plate and arrange the fish nicely on top. Garnish with dill.
7. Serve with boiled potatoes and dill butter, if desired.

Salmon-stuffed Perch Fillets with Roe Sauce

12 medium-sized fillets of perch
(approx. 600 g)
salt and freshly ground white pepper

Filling:
200 g fillet of salmon or rainbow trout,
diced
a pinch of cayenne pepper and
ground nutmeg
1 egg white
200 ml whipping cream
1 tbsp tomato purée
chopped dill and chives
100 ml fish stock
50 ml dry white wine

Sauce:
1/2 tbsp butter
3 tbsp chopped shallot
50 ml water
50 ml white wine vinegar
100 ml dry white wine
200 g unsalted butter, in small cubes
1 tsp lemon juice
salt and freshly ground white pepper
4 tbsp whipping cream, lightly whipped
3 tbsp whitefish roe

1. Season the diced salmon with salt, nutmeg and
cayenne pepper. Leave to stand for 15 minutes.
2. Mince the fish in a blender. Add the egg white
and cream gradually into the mixture.
3. Add the tomato purée, chopped dill and chives
and mix briefly in the blender.

4. Check the taste.
5. Spread the perch fillets onto a cutting board and
sprinkle with salt and white pepper.
6. Spoon the forcemeat into a piping bag (without a
nozzle) and pipe it onto half of the fillets.
7. Cover with rest of the fish fillets and press down.
8. Put the fish on a greased flat ovenproof dish.
9. Bring the stock and wine to boil and pour over
the fish.
10. Cover with foil and cook in a 200°C oven for
15-20 minutes.
11. Prepare the sauce. Melt the butter in a
saucepan. Sweat the chopped onion in it.
12. Pour in the water, vinegar and wine. Boil until
reduced by half.
13. Strain the sauce and pour back into the
saucepan. Whisk in the butter.
14. Just before serving fold in the roe and lightly
whipped cream. Serve with seasonal vegetables.

Salmon Wrapped in Savoy Cabbage with Beurre Blanc

200 g savoy cabbage
350 g fresh fillet of salmon or rainbow trout, cut in slices
200 g fillet of salmon or rainbow trout, diced
1 egg
100 ml whipping cream
1 tsp tomato purée
salt and freshly ground black pepper

Beurre Blanc:
2 tbsp finely chopped shallot
2 tbsp finely chopped fennel
1 tbsp butter for sweating
2 tbsp chopped parsley
1 tbsp chopped tarragon
50 ml white wine vinegar

100 ml dry white wine
100 ml water
200 g unsalted butter
1 tsp lemon juice
salt and freshly ground white pepper
1 tbsp chopped chervil
(3 tbsp lightly whipped cream)

1. Blanch the cabbage leaves in boiling salted water and rinse them briefly under cold water until cool.
2. Put the fish pieces in a blender and mince. Add the salt, cream, egg and tomato purée. Season with pepper.
3. Place the cabbage leaves onto a sheet of clingfilm, under which lies a sheet of foil.
4. Sprinkle pepper onto the sheets. Arrange the slices of salmon over the cabbage leaves and season with salt and pepper.

5. Spread the salmon mixture over the cabbage leaves. Gently roll the roulade up from one of the long edges, using the clingfilm and foil to help. First the film, then the foil.
6. Lift the roulade into an ovenproof dish with approx. 200 ml of warm water in it. Cook in a 175°C oven for 20-25 minutes.
7. Prepare the sauce. Sweat the chopped onions and fennel in butter. Add the herbs and liquids.
8. Simmer for about 10 minutes.
9. Liquidize in a blender and add the butter, bit by bit.
10. Heat up the sauce. Add the lemon juice, seasoning and chervil. The whipped cream can be added just before serving.
11. Cut the fish roulade into thin slices. Put the slices onto a plate, pour the sauce next to them and garnish with steamed seasonal vegetables.

Steamed Pikeperch with Saffron Sauce

4 fillets of pikeperch
1 tbsp butter
100 ml dry white wine
100 ml vegetable or fish stock
salt and freshly ground white pepper

Sauce:
3 tbsp chopped shallot
1/2 tbsp butter
200 ml shredded fennel
1 tsp saffron
50 ml water

50 ml white wine vinegar
200 g unsalted butter
1 tsp lemon juice
salt and freshly ground white pepper
(4 tbsp lightly whipped cream)

1. Sweat the shallot and fennel in butter in a saucepan.
2. Add the saffron and mix well.
3. Pour in the water, white wine vinegar and white vine. Boil until reduced by half.
4. Strain the sauce, season and keep warm.
5. Stir in the butter in small cubes.

6. Bring the cooking liquid for the fish to the boil. Arrange the fillets in an ovenproof dish and pour the liquid on top.
7. Cover the dish with foil and cook in a 200°C oven for 8-10 minutes, depending on the thickness of the fillets.
8. Fold the whipped cream into the sauce, if desired.
9. Pour a pool of sauce onto a plate and top with a fillet of fish. Serve with boiled potatoes and blanched vegetables.

Pikeperch Marinated in Sour Milk with Sabayon Sauce

4 fillets of pikeperch
salt and freshly ground white pepper
butter for frying

Marinade:
400 ml sour milk
1 garlic clove, crushed
1 tbsp Dijon mustard (unsweetened)
1 tbsp lemon juice
chives
dill

For coating:
flour
breadcrumbs

Sabayon sauce:
200 ml fish stock
50 ml lemon juice
6 egg yolks
salt and freshly ground white pepper
1 tbsp butter

1. Make the marinade and put the fish into it. Allow to marinate overnight.
2. Strain the fillets well and season with salt and white pepper.
3. Coat the fish fillets in a mixture of flour and breadcrumbs.
4. Fry in butter until nicely brown. (You can also simply brown the fish in the pan and cook it in the oven.)
5. Heat the fish stock and lemon juice.
6. Stir the egg yolks lightly in a pan. Whisk in the hot stock.
7. Allow to thicken. Add seasoning and butter. Serve immediately.

Game

Finland abounds in rabbits, waterfowl, fowl, deer and, to a lesser extent, large wild animals. Proportionally, it has more forests than any other European country. It possesses millions of hectares of swamps, groves, forests and waters. The hunter, however, cannot hunt wherever and whenever he pleases. The Finnish notion of a 'public right of access', also has its limits. The preservation of game and forestry are fortunately inseparable from nature conservation.

There is not enough game for the country's needs. The majority of game available in restaurants and stores has originally been farmed. This includes *reindeer, pheasants* and *geese.*

Reindeer (Rangifer tarandus fennicus) wander freely in nature during the summer months. In the autumn they're herded into pens and the owners round them up according to their marks. The reindeer eat vigorously and wholesomely in the woods all summer long. So reindeer meat is at its most succulent during the autumn slaughter. Reindeer meat is healthy and low in fat. In Lapland it's usually sautéed. Air-dried and smoked reindeer meat are also Lapp specialties. In the restaurants of southern Finland diners are treated to reindeer fillets, cutlets and tongue.

Elk (Alces alces) can be hunted with the permission of the game management area from September 30th to December 15th. Fresh venison is also available from meat counters during this period. It has a very low fat content and is ideal for stews, steaks, rolls, roasts and patées.

The elk is a large animal and often surprises tourists by coming very close to human habitats, including summer cottages and country homes. Elks can cause a great deal of grief, especially along the busy roads of southern Finland. This was one reason why as many as 26,000 hunting licenses were granted in 1995.

The number of forest birds has diminished. Those that are caught usually end up in the hunter's pot, without ever reaching the shop counter.

Willow grouse (Lagopus lagopus) was actually used as a fourth currency in northwest Lapland as recently as the 1930s. The Finnish mark, Swedish crown and Norwegian crown represented the official tender. Unfortunately, the willow grouse population has decreased to such an extent that all but a few hunters can make a living from hunting them. Nevertheless, it can still occasionally be found on Finnish menus.

Water fowl, such as *mallard* (Anas platyrhynchos) is more readily available. The wild duck hunting season is very long, starting on August 8th and closing on the last day of December. Wild duck can also be bought frozen from stores.

Shopkeepers supply game birds to those who want them. If you don't happen to have a friend who's into hunting, game dishes are always available in good restaurants all over Finland. Russian-style restaurants sometimes offer roast bear.

Hunting is strictly controlled all over the country by hunting clubs, game management areas and a variety of societies with vested interests. Each species is allocated its own rigidly monitored and specified hunting season, which varies from county to county.

Venison Stew

600 g joint of venison, diced
150 g onion, cut in half and sliced
180 g carrot, diced
180 g parsnip, diced
180 g celeriac, diced
juniper berries
fresh or dried rosemary
salt and freshly ground black pepper
3 tbsp balsamic vinegar

170 g (smoked) bacon
1 litre venison or ordinary stock
100 ml sour cream
2 tbsp blackcurrant jelly
3 tbsp blue cheese

Thickening:
100 ml whipping cream
4 tbsp flour

1. Put the meat, vegetables, crushed juniper berries, rosemary, seasoning and vinegar into a dish and mix thoroughly.
2. Cover with clingfilm and allow to marinate in the fridge overnight. Remove the meat, well in advance, and allow to stand at room temperature the following day.
3. Shred the bacon and transfer to a heated pot.
4. Brown the meat and vegetable cubes in batches together with the bacon.
5. Pour in the venison or ordinary stock and simmer for about 40 minutes.
6. Season with blackcurrant jelly. Add the thickening and sour cream. Simmer for a further 5-10 minutes. Sprinkle some crumbled blue cheese on top.
7. Serve the venison stew with, e.g. mashed root vegetables. Cook carrots (1/4), swede (1/4) and potatoes (1/2) and mash. Season with salt and a pinch of nutmeg.

Picture on previous spread (pages 30-31)

Reindeer with Rosemary and Chanterelles

300 g fillet of reindeer, cleaned
1 tbsp coarse salt
3 tsp rosemary, dried or fresh
freshly ground black pepper

Salad:
1 tbsp butter
200 ml sliced leek
1 litre fresh chanterelles, roughly chopped
3 tbsp sour cream
salt and freshly ground black pepper
50 ml chopped parsley
pink peppercorns

To garnish:
Lettuce leaves, fresh rosemary

1. Rub the salt and seasoning into the fillet. Grind the rosemary in a mortar or in your palm.
2. Wrap the fillet tightly in a plastic bag and leave to marinate in the fridge for about 4 hours.
3. Scrape the excess salt from the surface.
4. Wrap the fillet first in a clingfilm and then in a foil. Freeze for a minimum of 6 hours. Prepare the salad on the day you're serving the meat.
5. Sweat the sliced leek in butter. Add the chanterelles. Simmer until all the liquid has evaporated.
6. Add the sour cream and boil until thickened.
7. Season and add the parsley.
8. Make a bed from the lettuce leaves onto a serving plate and spoon the salad into the middle.
9. Cut thin slices from the frozen meat and arrange them around the mushroom salad.
10. Sprinkle pink peppercorns on top and decorate with a sprig of rosemary.

Traditional Finnish Wild Duck

2 wild ducks, oven-ready
salt
2 onions, cut in wedges
2 apples, cut in wedges
8 prunes
2 tbsp butter
thyme
rosemary
200 ml stock, seasoned with honey

Sauce:
2 tbsp butter
100 g vegetables for soup, diced
50 g champignons, sliced
1 tbsp blue cheese, crumbled
1 tbsp rowanberry jelly or red whortleberry jam
a small sprig of thyme
700 ml game or ordinary stock
2 tbsp flour
2 tbsp butter, whipped
2 tbsp cognac
100 ml whipping cream
salt and freshly ground white pepper

Serve with:
Chanterelles fried in butter and potato
wedges sprinkled with sesame seeds

Potato wedges:
4 raw potatoes, peeled and cut into
wedges
3 tbsp butter
2 tbsp sesame seeds
salt and freshly ground white pepper

1. Season the birds inside and out with salt.
2. Stuff the birds with onion and apple wedges and prunes.
3. Brown the birds thoroughly in butter and rub with the chopped herbs.

4. Place the ducks in an ovenproof dish, breast downwards and roast in the oven at 200°C.
5. Baste occasionally with the honeyed stock.
6. When the ducks have been in the oven for 20 minutes, turn them around and baste.
7. Cook in the oven for a further 25 minutes and check with a skewer. The ducks should remain slightly pink inside.
8. In the meantime, prepare the sauce and potatoes.
9. Melt the butter in a saucepan and sweat the diced vegetables and mushrooms in it.
10. Add the blue cheese, jelly, thyme sprig and stock.
11. Boil for about 15 minutes until the mixture is reduced to 500 ml.
12. Strain the sauce and pour back into the saucepan.
13. Mix the flour with the whipped butter. Whisk the thickening into the sauce. Simmer for 5 minutes. Remove from heat.
14. Melt the butter in a frying pan. Add the potatoes and fry for a while. Add the sesame seeds and brown. Season.

15. Lay the potatoes in an ovenproof dish and cook in a 200°C oven for about 10-15 minutes.
16. Cut the ducks into serving pieces and remove the bones.
17. Top off the sauce with cream, cognac and seasoning. Pour a pool of sauce onto a plate and arrange the duck and potatoes on it.

Willow Grouse with Pink Peppercorn Sauce

2 willow grouses, oven-ready
2 tbsp butter
salt and freshly ground black pepper

Sauce:
30 g butter
1 onion, chopped
rosemary
thyme
2 juniper berries
4 tbsp flour
500 ml game or ordinary stock
20 g blue cheese, diced
sugar and salt
500 ml whipping cream
20 ml cognac
pink peppercorns, crushed

1. Cut the breasts off the birds.
2. Make a stock from the carcasses.
3. Prepare the sauce. Sweat the onion in butter.
4. Add the herbs, juniper berries and flour.
Bring to the boil.
5. Add the game stock and blue cheese.
6. Simmer for 20 minutes, stirring occasionally.
7. Strain the sauce and return to the pan.
Add the cream, salt and sugar. Boil until thickened.
8. Add the cognac and pink peppercorns.
Check the taste.
9. Brown the willow grouse breasts in butter. Then
cook them for 5-8 minutes in an oven at 175°C.
The breasts should remain slightly pink inside.
Season with salt and pepper.
10. Cut the breasts into two lengthwise. Pour a
pool of the pink peppercorn sauce onto a plate
and arrange the breast on top.
11. Decorate with seasonal cooked vegetables
and serve with potato croquettes.

Willow grouse with pink peppercorn sauce

Roast fillet of reindeer with cranberry sauce

Roast Fillet of Reindeer with Cranberry Sauce

600 g fillet of reindeer
butter for frying
salt and freshly ground black pepper

Cranberry sauce:
1 tbsp butter
a total of 50 g of vegetables:
celeriac, parsnip, carrot, shallot, leek
100 ml cranberry juice
400 ml game or ordinary stock
2 tsp sugar
2 tbsp cornflour
a dash of red wine
freshly ground black pepper
freshly ground white pepper
sea salt

a total of 400 ml of raw vegetables
(e.g. turnip, celeriac, parsnip, potato,
carrot), cut into decorative pieces

To garnish:
cranberries
fresh sprigs of herb

1. First prepare the sauce. Sweat the finely chopped vegetables in butter in a saucepan.
2. Add the cranberry juice, stock and sugar. Simmer for about 20 minutes.
3. Strain the sauce and thicken with cornflour dissolved in red wine. Simmer for 5 minutes.
4. Cut the fillet of reindeer into 4 pieces and fry in a pan until medium.
5. Season the meat with salt and pepper.
6. Cut the pieces diagonally into slices.
7. Boil the vegetables "al dente".
8. Place them on a plate and arrange the meat on the bed of vegetables.
9. Surround with the sauce and cranberries. Garnish with a fresh sprig of herb.

Reindeer and Swede Roulade

400 g fillet of reindeer
300 g swede, cooked and mashed
200 g swede, blanched and diced
2 tbsp honey
4 tbsp breadcrumbs
2 egg yolks
salt and freshly ground black pepper

1. Clean the membranes off the fillet of reindeer and cut it horizontally so that the pieces stay intact.
2. Place the meat fillet onto a sheet of clingfilm under which lies a piece of foil. Press gently with fist until thinner. Season with salt and pepper.
3. Mix together the mashed and diced swedes, honey, breadcrumbs, egg yolks and seasoning.
4. Spread the mixture onto the meat and roll it up like a Swiss roll, first into the clingfilm and then into the foil.
5. Put some water in an ovenproof dish and transfer the roulade into it.
6. Roast for 15-20 minutes in a 200°C oven so that the meat remains slightly pink.
7. Serve with a strong dark game sauce and vegetables.

Potatoes and Cabbages

The potato is very much a staple of the Finnish dining table. It appears every day in one form or other. It's as important to Finns as rice is to China or pasta is to Italians.

Several sorts of potato are extremely suitable for cultivation in the Finnish soil, so there's a good selection for a variety of purposes. Floury varieties are ideal for making mashed or baked potatoes. Those of firmer consistency are suitable for use in salads and casseroles or as side dishes.

Lapland has its own potato, the *Puikula*, a lengthy, oval-shaped 'spud'. It's very sweet and floury and offers an excellent harvest under the warming light of a northern summer.

If Finns were to choose their number one potato, it would have to be 'new potatoes'. The appearance of so-called new potatoes in the market places is one of the highlights of the Finnish summer. A steaming saucepan full of dainty, sweet potatoes calls only for a sprinkling of chopped dill and a dab of butter. Dill and potato go side by side in Finland. Dill is also by far the most used herb in the Finnish kitchen. People from other cultures may find this hard to fathom since dill tends to be rather insipid in most parts of Europe. The secret to its success lies in the light. Dill grown in Finland's light summer nights develops a very strong aroma. Leafy dill is superb for potato and fish dishes. Flowering dill heads are a must for pickling cucumbers or boiling fresh-water crayfish. Dill seeds add a distinctive flavour to bread doughs.

Cabbages came to the Finnish kitchens by courtesy of Russia. *Sauerkraut* isn't widely used, but various other cabbage dishes are very popular. The most traditional of these is cabbage rolls. The first cabbages of summer are eagerly uprooted and the first succulent rolls are prepared as early as August. Making the best possible rolls, following a traditional precept, is extremely time-consuming but well worth the effort. First, the filling is prepared, either from rice or barley, mutton or beef and chopped cabbage. The cabbage leaves are stuffed, rolled up and fried in a pan. They're then transferred to an oven to cook, after having been glazed with golden syrup. Cabbage rolls are served with red whortleberries, pickled beetroot and cucumbers and our all-important potatoes.

It's impossible to find home-grown fresh vegetables in Finland during her bitterly-cold winter months. Never fear - Nature's here! Root vegetables - potatoes, carrots, celeriac, swede, parsnip, beetroot and cabbages maintain their sweet taste and vitamins thanks to the sanctuary of the Finnish cellar. Root vegetables add colour and variety to the winter dining-table. Freshly grated, they're either eaten as salads or used for flavouring bread doughs.

Potato Cake

10 medium-sized potatoes, peeled

2 eggs
200 ml sour cream
salt
3 garlic cloves, crushed
a pinch of nutmeg

Filling:
500 ml blanched or sweated mushrooms,
chopped (chanterelle, pickled mushrooms,
shiitake, champignon...)
100 ml chopped onion, sweated
100 ml chopped parsley

100 ml chopped basil
salt and freshly ground black pepper
100 ml grated Parmesan cheese
breadcrumbs

On top:
3 tomatoes
150 ml grated Black label Emmenthal

1. Boil the potatoes in salted water.
2. Mix together the eggs, sour cream, salt, garlic
and nutmeg.
3. Mash the cooked potatoes. Stir in the sour cream
and egg mixture.

4. Mix the filling ingredients together and check the
taste.
5. Grease a round 24-cm loose-bottom tin and
cover with breadcrumbs.
6. Spread half of the mashed potatoes in the tin.
7. Spread the filling on top and cover with the rest
of the mash.
8. Bake in a 200°C oven for about 40 minutes.
9. Blanch the tomatoes. Skin them, cut them into
wedges, remove the seeds and cut into strips.
10. Remove the cake from the oven. Spread the
tomato strips on top and sprinkle with grated
cheese. Gratinate in the oven for 10 minutes.
11. Remove the slightly cooled cake from the tin
and serve with fresh salad, or as a side dish.

Duchess Potatoes and Beetroots Cooked in Sour Cream

10 potatoes, cooked
50 g butter
3 egg yolks
2 tsp salt
freshly ground white pepper
nutmeg

Beetroots:
2 tbsp butter
800 ml fresh beetroot, diced
1 onion, finely chopped
400 ml sour cream
2 tbsp red wine vinegar

sugar
salt and freshly ground black pepper
fresh basil or parsley, chopped

1. Peel the potatoes and mash them. Add the butter.
2. Stir the egg yolks into the slightly cooled mash. Add the seasoning.
3. Put the mashed potatoes into a piping bag. Pipe neat "roses" onto the edges of a flat, ovenproof dish.
4. Sweat the diced beetroot and onion in butter.
5. Add the sour cream, wine vinegar and sugar.
6. Season with salt and pepper.
7. Gratinate the piped potato purée in the top layer of the oven until golden-brown; 250°C, for 6-8 minutes.

8. Spoon the cooked beetroot mixture into the dish and garnish with chopped basil or parsley.

Baked Potatoes with Mushroom Filling

4 baking potatoes

Filling:
2 tbsp butter
100 g fresh mushrooms, or 150 g frozen
(trumpet chanterelle, chanterelle, ceps,
shiitake, champignon...)
50 ml onion, finely chopped
50 ml whipping cream
salt and freshly ground black pepper
100 ml grated Black label Emmenthal

1. Bake the potatoes (in foil) in a 200°C oven, for 40-
60 minutes, depending on the size of the potatoes.
Prick with a skewer to see if done.
2. Remove the flesh from the baked potatoes. Leave
some on the sides so the potatoes don't collapse.
3. Chop the mushrooms and sweat them in the butter
with the onion.
4. Mash the potato flesh with a fork. Add the
mushroom and onion mixture, cream, chives and
seasoning.
5. Fill the potato skins and sprinkle with grated
cheese.
6. Gratinate for 15 minutes in a 175°C oven until hot
and nicely browned.

Baked Potatoes with Cold-smoked Whitefish

4 baking potatoes

Filling:
1 tbsp butter
50 ml chopped red onion
100 ml chopped leek
1 large garlic clove, crushed
100 ml blue cheese, grated

200 ml boneless cold-smoked whitefish,
cut into strips
freshly ground white pepper
100 ml grated cheese

1. Bake the potatoes (in foil) in a 200°C oven,
for 40-60 minutes, depending on the size of the
potatoes. Prick with a skewer to see if done.
2. Remove the flesh from the baked potatoes. Leave
some on the sides so the potatoes don't collapse.
3. Melt the butter in a pan. Add the onion, garlic
and leek.
4. Sweat them for a while. Add the blue cheese
and allow to melt.
5. Add the mashed, cooked potato flesh and the
cold-smoked whitefish. Season with white pepper.
6. Spoon the filling into the potato skins, sprinkle
with grated cheese and gratinate for 10 minutes in
a 200°C oven, until golden-brown. You can also
prepare the potatoes beforehand and heat them up
just before serving.

Potatoes with Cucumber and Dill

1 tbsp butter
100 ml finely chopped onion
1 tbsp capers
100 m finely diced fresh cucumber
200 ml whipping cream
6 medium-sized potatoes, cooked and
sliced
50 ml chopped dill
50 ml chopped chives
salt and freshly ground black pepper

1. Melt the butter in a large saucepan and sweat the
onion, capers and cucumber in it.
2. Add the cream and cook until the sauce thickens.
3. Add the potatoes and bring to the boil.
4. Season with dill, chives, salt and pepper. Serve.

Fried Creamy Potatoes

1 tbsp butter
600 g peeled potatoes, cut in wedges
200 ml finely chopped onion
3 garlic cloves, sliced
200 ml diced red bell pepper
200 ml vegetable stock
100 ml whipping cream
fresh herbs according to taste, e.g. basil
salt and freshly ground black pepper

1. Heat the butter in a pan and fry the potatoes in it.
Add the onion and garlic when the potatoes are
golden- brown.
2. Add the red bell pepper and stock.
3. Cover with a lid and simmer for about 10
minutes.
4. Add the cream and seasoning, bring to the boil
and serve.

Potato Terrine

1 tbsp oil
200 ml onion, finely chopped
1.5 kg peeled potatoes, cut into strips
300 g grated Black label Emmenthal
1/2 tbsp dried thyme
salt and freshly ground black pepper
400 ml sour cream
300 ml milk
7 eggs

1. Sweat the onions in oil in a frying pan and allow
to cool.
2. Mix together the potato strips, grated cheese,
sweated onions and seasoning.
3. Press the mixture tightly into a long,
large bread tin.
4. Mix together milk, eggs and sour cream and pour
over the potatoes in the tin.
5. Bake the terrine in a 175°C oven for about
1-1 1/2 hours. Tip out to serve.

Cabbage Roulade

200 g cabbage leaves
(Chinese cabbage, head cabbage, savoy
cabbage)
2 tbsp oil
100 ml onion, finely chopped
200 ml carrot, finely diced
200 ml blanched or sweated mushrooms
(shiitake, chanterelle, etc.),
400 ml cabbage, finely chopped
200 ml courgette, finely chopped
100 ml crushed tomatoes
200 ml cooked crushed pearl barley or
lentils
salt and freshly ground black pepper

1. Trim off the tough stalks from the cabbage leaves.
2. Blanch the leaves in boiling water. Cool briefly under cold running water and drain.
3. Sweat the onion, carrot, mushrooms, cabbage and courgette in the oil.
4. Add the tomatoes and seasoning and bring to the boil.
5. Stir in the cooked pearl barley or lentils.
6. Arrange the cabbage leaves onto a sheet of foil or greaseproof paper. Sprinkle them with a little salt and black pepper.
7. Spread the stuffing on one edge of the leaves and roll up, like a Swiss roll. Wrap a sheet of foil around the roll and close the ends tightly.
8. Transfer into an ovenproof dish, add some hot water and cook in a 200°C oven for about 20 minutes.

Traditional Stuffed Cabbage Rolls

1 large head cabbage
2-3 tbsp butter
1-2 tbsp golden syrup

Stuffing:
50 ml brown or polished rice
200 ml meat stock
300 g lean minced mutton
shredded cabbage
100 ml whipping cream
1 egg yolk (use the white for sealing the rolls)
salt and white pepper

1. Cook the rice in the stock until half-done.
2. Cut off the stem of the cabbage. Blanch the cabbage in slightly salted water. Remove the leaves as soon as they start to separate.
3. Save the bigger leaves for the rolls. Trim off any tough pieces and shred the smaller leaves ready for the stuffing.
4. Mix the ingredients of the stuffing together until smooth. Thin with some cooking water from the cabbage, if necessary.
5. Place some stuffing in each leaf, fold them up, parcel-like, and seal with the egg white. The rolls should be small and thin.
6. Brown the rolls in the butter in a frying pan. Pack them into an ovenproof dish.
7. Rinse the pan with some cooking water from the cabbage and pour into the oven dish.
8. Pour a thin strip of syrup over the rolls and cook in a 175°C oven for about 1 1/2 hours. Turn them once and add more cooking water, if required.
9. Add a drop of cream before serving to act as a sauce.

Mushrooms

Three out of every five Finns go berry- or mushroom-picking. Probably the nicest aspect of these outdoor pursuits is the delight of coming across a good spot. It's a little like hunting for treasure. If the summer hasn't been too dry and the autumn not too cold, then the woods can be teeming with mushrooms. So much so that you'd better watch where you tread. Berries and mushrooms are at their most plentiful from the end of July until the beginning of November.

In Finland anyone is allowed to pick mushrooms or berries more or less anywhere, including private land and national parks, just as long as you follow the country code. There's plenty of accessible forest land in Finland so, in theory, there shouldn't be any need to go sniffing around other people's property. But if you do find yourself on private land all you have to do is ask for permission from the folk who own it.

Mushrooms absorb dust and dirt easily, so it's not advisable to pick them near roads, factories or city parks.

Finland's annual mushroom yield is estimated to be somewhere in the region of 2,000 to 5,000 million kilos. There are two thousand different varieties of mushrooms, some five hundred of which are edible. About ninety of these are considered suitable as food or for cooking purposes. But in terms of popularity the number boils down to a kind of mushroom 'top ten'. It's advisable only to pick those mushrooms you recognize for sure. There are roughly fifty poisonous varieties that lurk in the Finnish forests. And around a dozen of these are lethal.

From the end of July onwards, market place tables buckle under the weight of *chanterelles* (Cantharellus cibarius). It's easy to prepare, golden yellow in colour and mild in taste. Three good reasons for it being Finland's most popular mushroom.

Several varieties of *boleti* grow in Finland. *Cep* (Boletus edulis) is the most sought-after.

The tradition of preparing *milk caps* originates from the Russian kitchen. Slightly sharp-tasting, they are mostly used in mushroom salads.

Sheep Polyporus (Scutiger ovinus) is as nutritious as veal and therefore a staple mushroom for all Finnish mushroom-pickers.

Mushrooms also contain more fibre than carrots or wheat bran.

The *false morel* (Gyromitra esculenta) season starts in early spring. This mushroom gives off a superb aroma. But beware: it's extremely poisonous when fresh. The poison only dissipates through boiling. After cleaning, morels have to be cooked twice for about five minutes (3 litres of water per 1 litre of mushrooms). The water should be discarded after both boilings. After boiling, the mushrooms should then be thoroughly rinsed for a reasonable time under ample cold running water. Even dried morels have to treated in the same way before they can be considered ready for use.

The kitchen should be aired during the boiling procedure. All this may sound rather off-putting, but the result of all this painstaking work will be a supremely aromatic and delicious ingredient for sauces and soups.

There are plenty of well-organized and guided mushroom trips to go on in the autumn. And mushroom clubs spring up all over the country at exactly the right time. Many of these clubs offer mushroom recognition courses - "Mind that toadstool, Ms!"

False Morel and Chanterelle Terrine

Jelly:
100 ml vegetable stock
100 ml white wine
2 leaves gelatin, soaked in cold water
salt and freshly ground black pepper
100 ml finely chopped red onion
100 ml finely chopped chives

False morel jelly:
2 tbsp butter
400 ml chopped false morels*
50 ml chopped onion
50 ml chopped leek
100 ml white wine
4 leaves gelatin, soaked in cold water
a pinch of sugar
salt and freshly ground black pepper
300 ml whipping cream, whipped

*After cleaning, boil the false morels twice
for about 5 minutes (3 litres of water per
1 litre of mushrooms).
Discard the water after both boilings.
Rinse thoroughly for a reasonable time
under ample cold running water.

Chanterelle jelly:
2 tbsp butter
400 ml chopped chanterelles
100 chopped red onion
200 ml sour cream
4 leaves gelatin, soaked in cold water
salt and freshly ground black pepper
1 tbsp pink peppercorns
100 ml whipping cream, whipped

To garnish:
chives

Cep Tartare

400 g fresh or frozen ceps
50 ml finely chopped onion
50 ml finely chopped chives
50 ml finely chopped fresh basil
or other fresh herbs according to taste
50 ml olive oil
50 ml balsamic vinegar
salt and freshly ground black pepper

To garnish:
6 tsp roe (e.g. whitefish roe)
green asparagus
radish strips

1. Chop the mushrooms extremely finely.
2. Mix the mushrooms with the chopped onions
and herbs.
3. Add the oil, balsamic vinegar, black pepper
and salt.
4. Form into "tartare steaks" about 2 cm thick.
5. Serve on a plate and garnish with, e.g. blanched
asparagus and radish strips.
6. Surround with sauce made with "kermaviili" or
plain yoghurt, seasoned with mustard and herbs or
herbs and lemon juice.

1. Line a 1.5 litre bread tin with clingfilm. Sprinkle the onions onto the bottom of the tin.
2. Bring the vegetable stock and white wine to the boil. Add the softened gelatin.
3. Pour 100 ml of jelly into the tin. Chill.
4. Prepare the false morel jelly. Melt the butter in a saucepan. Sweat the false morels in it. Add the onions and sweat.
5. Pour in the white wine. Simmer for 5 minutes.

Stir in the softened gelatin. Add the seasoning and leave to cool.
6. Fold in the whipped cream.
7. Spoon the jelly into the tin and on the sides. Leave a hollow in the middle for the other jelly. Chill.
8. Prepare the chanterelle jelly. Melt the butter in a saucepan. Sweat the chanterelles for a while, then add the onions and sweat.

9. Mix in the sour cream and simmer for 5 minutes. Stir in the softened gelatin. Add the seasoning and leave to cool.
10. Fold in the whipped cream.
11. Spoon the jelly in the tin. Chill for 30 minutes.
12. Decorate the top of the jelly with chives, if desired. Pour the rest of the jelly on top. Leave to set until the next day.

Trumpet Chanterelle and Roe Roulade

Mushroom roulade:
1 tbsp butter
50 ml chopped onion
200 ml fresh trumpet chanterelles, finely chopped
200 ml single cream
1 egg yolk
2 whole eggs
salt and freshly ground white pepper

Filling:
50 ml whipping cream
3 leaves gelatin
50 ml chopped dill
1 tbsp chopped onion
200 ml sour cream
100 ml whitefish roe (or other fish roe)
salt and freshly ground black pepper

1. Sweat the onion and mushrooms in the butter, add the cream and leave to cool.
2. Add the egg yolk and eggs. Season with salt and pepper.
3. Spoon the mixture into a greased square tin or a baking sheet so that it's about 1/2 cm thick.
4. Bake in a 160°C oven for about 10 minutes.
5. Turn the roulade out onto a sheet of greaseproof paper and leave to cool. In the meanwhile, make the filling.
6. Heat the cream and add the gelatin, soaked in cold water. Leave to cool.
7. Mix the rest of the ingredients together. Add the cream and gelatin mixture and check the taste.
8. Spread the filling over the mushroom roulade and roll up from one of the long edges with the help of the greaseproof paper.
9. Leave to set in the fridge for about 2 hours.
10. Cut into slices and serve on a bed of salad.

Mushroom and Whitefish Roe Sandwich

4 slices rye bread, crusts removed,
10 x 7 cm in size
1 tbsp butter
100 g whitefish roe, drained

Mushroom salad:
200 ml chopped milk caps
2 tbsp chopped leek
1 tbsp chopped red onion
1 tbsp oil
salt and freshly ground black pepper
100 ml sour cream, whipped

To garnish:
red onion strips

1. Combine the mushrooms, leek, onion, oil and seasoning.
2. Spoon the whipped sour cream in a piping bag.
3. Butter the bread slices. Cover the slices diagonally, half with roe and half with the mushroom salad.
4. Pipe sour cream in the middle and garnish with red onion strips.

Trumpet chanterelle and roe roulade

Mushroom Salad and Blinis

Blinis (12 small ones):
5 g = 1 tsp fresh yeast
150 ml warm milk
100 ml buckwheat flour
50 ml plain flour
50 ml "kermaviili" or plain yoghurt
1 egg yolk
salt
1 egg white, whisked

Mushroom salad:
600 ml chopped pickled mushrooms (milk caps or ceps)
50 ml chopped leek
50 ml chopped red onion
50 ml chopped parsley
a pinch of sugar
salt and freshly ground black pepper
100 ml sour cream, whipped

1. Make the mushroom salad. Mix the mushrooms, leek, onion and parsley together. Add the seasoning and fold in the whipped sour cream.
2. Prepare the blinis. Dissolve the yeast in the warm milk. Add the flours, "kermaviili", egg yolk and salt.
3. Mix the batter until smooth. Leave to stand for at least 30 minutes in room temperature.
4. Fold the whisked egg white into the batter just before frying.
5. Fry the blinis in butter on both sides over a low heat in a pancake pan.
6. Serve hot with the mushroom salad.

Mushroom salad and blinis

Chanterelle Soup

3 tbsp butter
50 ml chopped onion
400 g fresh chanterelles, chopped
(or 150 g canned)
3 tbsp plain flour
800 ml vegetable stock
200 ml whipping cream
salt and freshly ground black pepper
50 ml chopped parsley

1. Sweat the onion and mushrooms in butter.
2. Stir in the flour. Pour in the vegetable stock, continuously stirring.
3. Simmer for 15 minutes.
4. Add the seasoning and cream. Bring to the boil.
5. Sprinkle the parsley on top just before serving.
6. Serve with toast and butter.

Mushroom Bake

3 tbsp butter
1 onion
500 ml mushrooms
250 g mutton or reindeer, minced
100 ml red wine
fresh thyme
2 garlic cloves, crushed
250 ml sour cream
approx. 150 g rye bread slices, crusts removed
salt and freshly ground black pepper

1. Clean the fresh mushrooms and blanch if necessary. Soak the dried or pickled mushrooms.
2. Sweat the mushrooms in butter and season with salt and pepper. Put them aside.
3. Sweat the onions. Add the minced meat and fry.
4. Pour in the wine. Simmer for a while and season with garlic, salt, pepper and thyme.
5. Grease an ovenproof dish with butter and cover the bottom with the bread slices.
6. Spread the onions on top, then the meat and, finally, the mushrooms.
7. Season the sour cream with salt and pepper and spread on top. Cook in a 175°C oven for about 45 minutes.

Bread

Every country has its own traditions of making bread. Finland is no exception. Originally, the country was divided into two permanent areas of habitation: the east and the west. Both geographical areas developed their own regional kitchens. The eastern area was influenced by Slavic culture, the western by Germanic.

The traditional Finnish cottage in the east had an oven which was heated up on a daily basis during the winter. Food was prepared in clay pots in the oven, the meat was cured in a wooden trough and bread, pies and pasties were baked whenever the need arose. Soft rye bread was the daily bread of the east, an area where the preparation of food relied heavily on the oven.

In western regions the cottage was heated by a fireplace and the food cooked in a three-legged pot or a pan hanging over the fire. Outside, there was usually a separate little hut for baking bread, often huge quantities at a time. Baking days were in the autumn and the spring. The breads, which were usually circular with a hole in the middle, were dried and hung on poles that stretched across the ceiling. The bread of the west was dry rye bread, which was soaked before eating.

Rye bread still plays an important role in Finland's impressive range of breads. It's also the bread that Finns most long for when they're abroad. Its strong taste is easy to get used to. Its appearance and degree of sourness vary from region to region.

Some like it sour and some do not,
Some like it oven-fresh
With butter on the top.
Some like it crisp and some like it cold
And many say it tastes the best
A few days old.

Many Finns also eat rye bread at breakfast. It definitely fills you up more than the instant 'emptiness' of white bread. The best rye bread is still baked in a wood-fired baking oven. The rye grains are carefully ground in a stone mill. Only water, salt and sourdough root are then added into the flour. The root could well be over a hundred years old in the countryside.

Rye has now been scientifically proven as being beneficial for maintaining and improving people's health. It's also more suitable here for cultivation than wheat. In the old days, when children were sent out from remote country houses into the big wide world, rye bread and sour milk, the staples of the Finnish diet, were always included in the rucksack.

Karelian Rice Pasties

The Karelian rice pasty is a significant representative of the Finnish baking tradition. They're the hamburgers or pizzas of Finland. Originally, they were a specialty of eastern Finland. But they gradually spread throughout the rest of the country. Most of them, however, are eaten in the provinces of Savonia and Karelia, situated near Finland's eastern border. Housewives and bakeries compete for who can make the best and most authentic pasties.

People are also still arguing over the original shape of the pasty. Karelian pasties comprise a thin rye dough crust with a filling made of rice pudding, carrot and rice or mashed potato. The pasties really should be eaten while fresh. The ideal place to bake them in is a stone baking oven. They're at their most scrumptious straight out of the oven, crisp and hot enough for the egg and butter spread to melt on top.

Barley Loaf

500 ml milk
50 g fresh yeast
1 tsp salt
500 ml barley flour
400 ml plain flour

1. Heat the milk until warm and dissolve
the yeast in it.
2. Add the salt and flours.
3. Knead the dough until it's smooth and supple.
4. Let the dough rise until doubled in size.
5. Knead the dough for a moment.
Divide into 4 parts.
6. Shape into round breads on greaseproof
paper on a baking sheet.
7. Allow to rise in a warm place for 30 minutes.
Bake in a 225°C oven for 20-30 minutes.

Potato Bread

250 ml mashed potatoes
1/2 tsp salt
1 egg
150 ml unbleached flour
100 ml barley flour

1. Mix the mashed potatoes together with salt,
egg and flours.
2. Sprinkle some flour on greaseproof paper.
3. Divide the dough into two and pat into two
thin breads.
4. Prick the breads with a fork and bake
in a 275°C oven for 15-20 minutes.
5. Eat the bread warm, topped with egg and
butter spread.

Rye Bread

Sourdough root:
3 slices rye bread, without crusts
(or 1 tbsp sourdough)
1 litre water
1 litre rye flour

The next day:
30 g fresh yeast, dissolved in water
2 tbsp salt
1.5 litres rye flour

1. Crumble the bread and put into a large mixing
bowl. Pour in the warm water and mix. Stir in the
rye flour.
2. Cover the bowl with a cloth and leave the dough
root to stand at room temperature for 24 hours, until
bubbly and pungent.
3. Add the salt and yeast. Add the rye flour and
knead until smooth and firm.
4. Let the dough rise until doubled. This takes
longer than with ordinary yeast bread.
5. Divide the dough into 3 pieces and leave a small
part for the next dough. (Use that as the sourdough
root. Freeze it and soak it in warm water, then
proceed as normal according to the recipe.)
6. Shape into loaves and allow to rise under a cloth.
Bake in a 200°C oven for about 1 hour.

Finnish Spiced Loaf

(4-5 loaves)

Stage I
300 ml boiling water
200 ml malts
200 ml sugar

1. Pour the hot water over the malts and sugar. Allow to stand overnight.

Stage II
1 litre sour milk
5 tsp salt
75 g fresh yeast
200 ml puréed apple
2 tbsp caraway seeds
1 litre rye flour

1. Dissolve the yeast in warm sour milk. Add the malt mixture, salt, apple purée, caraway seeds and rye flour.
2. Allow to stand for about 3 hours, stirring occasionally.

Stage III
150 ml treacle
150 ml sugar
400 ml rye flour
approx. 1.9 litres white flour

1. Add the rest of the ingredients to the dough root, mix and leave to rise for an hour.
2. When the dough has risen, knead and shape into 4-5 loaves. Allow to rise for about 30 minutes.
3. Bake the breads in a 150°C oven for 2 hours. Brush with a mixture of water and treacle and bake for a further 30 minutes.

Karelian Rice Pasties

(makes about 25)

Rice mixture:
500 ml water
2 tbsp butter
250 ml short-grain glutinous rice
1 litre milk
1 1/2 tsp salt

Rye dough:
30 ml rye flour
150 ml plain flour
1 tsp salt
200 ml water

To glaze:
50 g butter
100 ml milk

1. Put the water and butter in a saucepan. Bring to the boil and stir in the rice.
2. Simmer for 10 minutes, stirring occasionally.
3. Add the milk and stir until boiling. Simmer for about 50 minutes, until the rice is done. Season with salt. Set aside to cool.
4. Mix the flours, salt and water together. Knead into a dough.
5. Roll the dough on a floured surface until about 2 mms thick.
6. Using a cutter, cut into circles of 8 cms in diameter.
7. Roll the circles into thin crusts. A pasta machine can also be used. Use flour to help in the rolling.
8. Fill the crusts with a thin layer of the rice mixture. Turn in 1 cm of the side to create an edge and pinch the edges.
9. Bake the pasties in a 300°C oven for 15-20 minutes.
10. Brush with butter and milk mixture and transfer to soften under a greaseproof paper and towel.
11. Eat hot with egg and butter spread (recipe on page 84).

Vegetable Cake
(one 24-26 cm round tin)

Pastry:
150 g butter
100 g grated cheese
250 ml flour
1 tsp baking powder
50 ml whipping cream

Filling:
800 g carrots, sliced
4 eggs
1 onion, chopped
200 ml sour cream
100 ml whipping cream
salt and freshly ground black pepper
500 ml broccoli heads

To garnish:
Various blanched vegetables according to taste: baby carrots, broccoli, spring onion, red onion, etc.

Jelly:
200 ml vegetable stock
2 leaves gelatin, softened in cold water

1. Cook the carrots and onion in 200 ml boiling water, in a covered saucepan.
2. Mash the vegetables and allow to cool.
3. Prepare the pastry bottom. Mix the butter, grated cheese, dry ingredients and cream lightly together.
4. Line a greased loose-bottom flan tin with the pastry and bake blind for 10 minutes in a 175°C oven.
5. Season the vegetable mixture with salt and pepper. Whisk in the eggs.
6. Add the sour cream and whipping cream.
7. Put the broccoli heads and vegetable mixture into the base of the flan.
8. Bake in a 175°C oven for approx. 1 1/4 hours.
9. Allow the cake to cool and decorate with blanched and/or fresh vegetables according to taste. Lay them in groups on top of the cake. Dissolve the gelatin in the stock and jelly the cake top with it.
10. Serve at room temperature with, e.g. crème fraîche and herb dressing.

Fish and Shrimp Cake

For the bottom:
1 1/2 cm thick disk cut from
a few-days-old round white bread,
without crust

For moistening:
50 ml vegetable broth

Filling:
500 g cold-smoked salmon
without bones, diced
100 ml chopped onion, sweated
1 tbsp chili sauce
400 ml crème fraîche
100 ml chopped dill
100 ml chopped chives
4 leaves gelatin, softened in cold water
salt and freshly ground black pepper

To garnish:
400 g cooked shrimps, peeled
tomato strips, scalded
lemon balm leaves

1. Line a round 22-cm loose-based cake tin with clingfilm. Put the bread on the bottom and moisten.
2. Mince the fish in a blender. Add the onion, chili sauce and crème fraîche. Mix until smooth.
3. Add the softened gelatin and stir thoroughly.
4. Add the dill, chives and seasoning.
5. Pour the filling into the tin and allow to set for about 2 hours in the fridge.
6. Arrange the shrimps neatly on top of the fish mousse and garnish with tomato strips and herbs.
7. Serve with, e.g. chili and tomato sauce.

Traditional Finnish Buns

500 ml milk
2 tsp salt
200 ml caster sugar
1 tbsp cardamum
1.2 - 1.4 litres plain white flour
2 sachets dry yeast (22 g) or
50 g fresh yeast
200 g butter or margarine
1 egg for glazing

1. Make sure that all the ingredients are at room temperature.
2. Dissolve salt, sugar and cardamum into warm (37°C) milk. If dry yeast is used, the milk should be hot (42°C).
3. Mix the dry yeast with the flour. Add the flour and yeast mixture gradually into the liquid. The fresh yeast must be dissolved into the milk.
4. Set aside approx. 200 ml flour. It should be added at the very end.
5. Knead the dough for a while to improve elasticity.
6. Finally, add the softened butter or margarine and continue kneading until the dough is smooth. Add the rest of the flour, if necessary.
7. When making small buns, the dough can be softer than when making a twist.
8. Place the dough in a bowl, tightly cover with an oiled sheet of clingfilm and allow to rise until doubled in size.
9. Shape into buns and/or twists.
10. Brush the swollen buns with beaten egg and sprinkle with coarse sugar, caster sugar, and/or almond flakes.
11. Bake buns in a hot oven, 225°C for 10-15 minutes and twists in a 200°C oven for 20-25 minutes, according to size.

Ginger Snaps

500 g butter
400 g caster sugar
200 ml golden syrup
2 tsp ground cinnamon
4 tsp ground cloves
1 tsp ground orange peel
5 tsp bicarbonate of soda
approx. 1 kilo plain white flour
4 eggs

1. Bring the butter, sugar, syrup and spices to the boil. Allow to cool.
2. Add the bicarbonate of soda to the cool mixture and mix well.
3. Beat in the eggs one by one and mix well.
4. Add the flour, mixing continuously. The dough can be fairly hard.
5. Leave the dough overnight in the fridge. Always bake a test biscuit before rolling out a larger batch. Add some flour if necessary.
6. Roll out the pastry. Cut into shapes using biscuit cutters.
7. Bake in a 225°C oven for about 6 minutes. Keep an eye on them so they won't burn!
8. Cool on a wire rack and decorate with icing (400 ml icing sugar/1 egg white), if desired.

Milk and Cheese

Finnish cows are just as delighted as the rest of us when summer arrives. As soon as it's warm enough they're set free to roam the lush green pastures. It's great fun to witness their initial open-air frolics. Calves have to be lead around on leashes so they don't break their frail legs in all the excitement. There's plenty of clean grass and good clear water in the meadows, so Finnish cows eat and drink well. That's why their milk is regarded the purest in Europe. Cows graze from the end of May until early September, only lumbering into the shed at milking time.

Milk has long been regarded as the nectar of Finland. There are many kinds of milk and it's still a great favourite at the food table. There's also an impressive array of sour milk products. Piimä, which is basically soured milk, is very popular. As a drink, it acts as a thick and sourish thirst-quencher, but it can also add an essential taste to bread and cake doughs.

Viili is only found in Finland. It's a fermented milk product, eaten either as a snack or at breakfast, akin to yoghurt for consumption. Viili is devoured in great amounts during the summer months. It cools you down and provides you with just enough nutrition for the heat of the summer. It can also be prepared at home quite easily. All you need is a spoonful of viili as a 'starter', and pour some tepid milk on top. It's ready in a few hours and can then be transferred to the fridge to cool.

Curd cheese and sour cream originated in the Russian kitchen. Basic curd cheese contains no fat. It's ideal for Finnish berries, pies and pastries as well as an ingredient for ice cream.

Sour cream is a sour milk product which boasts a high fat content. It offers a soft taste to sauces and stews. It's a 'must' for serving Finnish roes. Here's the secret: fish roe, finely chopped onion and whipped sour cream are mixed together, seasoned with white pepper and served with baked potatoes, toast or blinis - "yummy".

Lammi's Black label Emmenthal is Finland's most famous cheese. It has won top prizes in international cheese competitions. Kainuu's baked bread cheese is a perfect example of the Finnish tradition of cheese-making. It's prepared in a variety of ways, depending on the area.

Butter has also enjoyed a long standing in the Finnish kitchen. There are wide varieties of butters for a wide range of uses. Butter is often used in place of sauce for flavouring foods. A dab of salted butter is all that early potatoes and vegetables need. Rye bread tastes best spread with butter. The simplest and perhaps best sauce for Finnish fish is a spoonful or two of melted, freshly-churned butter. Loose butter is sold in indoor markets.

A glass of cold milk, a slice of buttered rye bread or a warm bun, freshly baked at home - Finnish fast food at its best!

Egg and Butter Spread

100 g butter
3 hard-boiled eggs, mashed
50 ml chopped parsley

1. Mix the soft butter with the eggs and parsley.
2. Serve at room temperature. Goes well with Karelian rice pasties, unleavened bread and scones.

Home-made Cheese

5 litres milk
1.7 litres sour milk
5 eggs
100 ml chopped herbs
(to taste, e.g: chopped nuts, ground pepper, diced bell pepper, chopped mint, parsley or garlic)

1. Warm the milk in a heavy-bottomed saucepan until it reaches 80°C.
2. Mix the sour milk with the eggs.
3. Pour the mixture into the milk and stir carefully.
4. When the cheese begins to thicken, sprinkle the herbs or seasoning on top. Stir lightly into the cheese.
5. Remove from the heat, cover with a lid and allow to stand for about 20 minutes.
6. Lift the cheese curd with a slotted spoon into a cheese mould or a sieve lined with a damp cheesecloth.
7. Put a weight on top and allow to drain overnight. Then turn out of the mould.

Baked Whey Cheese with Berry Coulis

3 litres whole milk
1 litre sour milk
2 eggs

For the cheese mixture:
2 1/2 eggs, beaten
1/2 tbsp salt

To glaze:
1/2 egg

1. Heat the milk in a large saucepan until boiling.
2. Beat the eggs lightly. Pour the sour milk into the beaten eggs.
3. Pour the sour milk and egg mixture into the hot milk, stirring continuously. Bring the mixture to the boil. Remove from heat and cover with a lid.
4. Leave the saucepan in a warm place for about 30 minutes. Cut the curd cross-ways. Let the whey separate for a while.
5. Lift the cheese curd with a slotted spoon into a cheese mould or a sieve lined with a damp cheesecloth.
6. Stir in the salt and beaten eggs. Fold the cheesecloth over to cover. Place a light weight on top.
7. Leave to drain overnight in the fridge.
8. Turn the cheese over to an ovenproof dish and glaze with beaten egg.
9. Bake in a 225°C oven for 15-20 minutes, until golden-brown. Serve warm with a berry coulis.

Curd Cheese with Bilberry Sauce

Sponge cake:
4 eggs
100 ml caster sugar
200 ml plain flour
1/2 tsp baking powder

Filling:
750 g low-fat curd cheese or quark
5 eggs
250 ml sugar
100 g butter, melted

Bilberry sauce:
500 ml bilberries
500 ml water
100 ml sugar
1 1/2 tbsp cornflour

1. Drain the curd cheese or quark overnight in a sieve (use the whey for bread or bun dough).
2. Put the eggs, sugar, curd, and lastly the melted butter into a saucepan.
3. Heat up and thicken until the mixture becomes grainy.
4. Pour into a sieve lined with a dampened cheesecloth and strain overnight. Make the sponge cake. Whisk the eggs and sugar until pale and fairly stiff.
5. Sift in the flour with the baking powder and mix gently but thoroughly.
6. Spread onto a baking sheet which has been covered with greaseproof paper and bake in a 200°C oven for 10 minutes. Allow to cool.
7. Boil the bilberries, water and sugar in a saucepan.
8. Add the cornflour dissolved in some water and boil for a further 5 minutes.
9. Strain the sauce and leave to cool.
10. Spread the strained curd mixture onto the sponge cake. Cut out small shapes with a knife or a biscuit cutter.
11. Pour a pool of sauce onto a plate and top with the curd cheese pastry.

Finnish Blue Cheese Pie with Blackcurrant Sauce

Base:
125 g digestive biscuits, ginger snaps or
oatmeal biscuits
50 g unsalted butter, melted

Filling:
300 ml apple juice
4 egg yolks
100 ml sugar
100 g blue cheese
5 leaves gelatin
300 ml whipping cream

Jelly for decorating:
100 ml apple juice
1 leaf gelatin, softened in cold water

Sauce:
500 ml sweetened blackcurrant juice
1 tbsp potato flour

1. Crush the biscuits and add the melted butter.
2. Mix until smooth and press firmly into the base
of a round 24-cm loose-bottom cake tin.
3. Bring the juice and sugar to the boil.
4. Beat the egg yolks lightly and add the hot juice,
stirring continuously.
5. Allow the mixture to thicken over heat. Add the
cheese and the gelatin, softened in cold water.
Allow to cool.
6. Add the whipped cream to the cool mixture.
7. Pour the filling on top of the crumb crust and
allow to set.
8. Prepare the jelly. Dissolve the gelatin in warm
apple juice. Cool for a moment.
9. Pour the jelly over the set blue cheese mousse.
10. Leave to set in a cool place for 1 hour.
11. Prepare the sauce. Bring the blackcurrant juice
to the boil in a saucepan and add the potato flour,
dissolved in a small amount of water. Remove from
the heat and allow to cool until it reaches room
temperature.

Cheese Soufflé

50 g butter
50 ml flour
400 ml milk
5 egg yolks
5 egg whites
freshly ground black pepper
1/2 tsp salt
400 ml grated Black label Emmenthal

1. Melt the butter in a saucepan. Add the flour
and milk.
2. Stir until smooth and cook for a few minutes.
3. Remove the saucepan from the heat and beat
in the cheese, seasonings and egg yolks.
4. Whisk the egg whites until stiff. Gently fold
into the cheese mixture.
5. Pour the mixture into a well-greased soufflé dish,
a straight-sided casserole dish or into 4 ramekins.
6. Bake in the bottom of the oven at 150°C for
1 hour. Don't open the oven during the baking.
7. Serve immediately with fresh mixed salad.

Cheese and Beef Stew

3 tbsp oil
500 g fillet of beef, cut into strips
200 ml chopped shallots
200 ml bell pepper, cut into strips
2 tbsp flour
300 ml stock
200 ml red wine
50 ml small pickled onions, in slices
2 tbsp blackcurrant jelly
100 g Black label Emmenthal, finely diced
50 g blue cheese, diced

1. Fry the meat strips in hot oil. Put them aside on a plate.
2. Sweat the onion for a moment. Add the bell pepper strips.
3. Stir the flour into the vegetable mixture.
4. Add the stock and red wine. Boil until thickened.
5. Add the pickled onions and blackcurrant jelly. Bring to the boil.
6. Finally, add the cooked meat strips and diced cheese. Heat up and serve, e.g. with pasta.

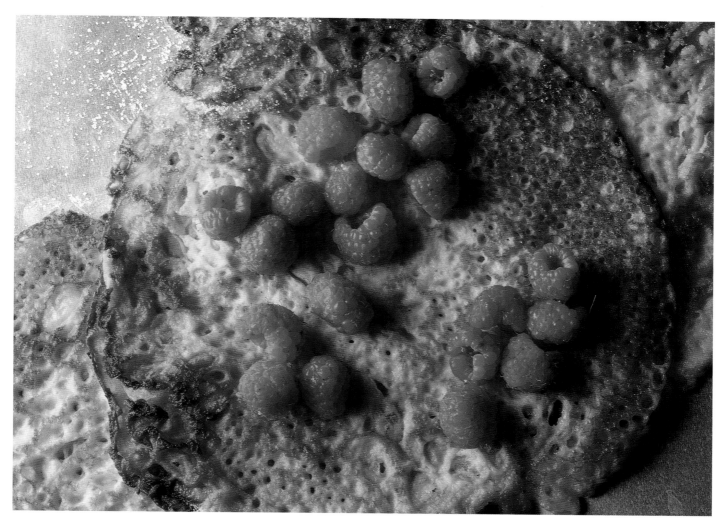

Finnish Pancakes

300 ml milk
2 eggs
200 ml plain flour
2 tbsp oil or melted butter
salt
(sugar)
butter or oil for frying

1. Pour the milk into a bowl. Add the flour and seasoning. Mix until smooth.
2. Add the eggs and oil or the melted butter, slightly cooled.
3. Heat the grease in a frying pan and pour in some batter.
4. Cook the pancake until set and golden-brown. Flip the pancake over and cook the other side.
5. Serve with jam, whipped cream, berries, cinnamon and sugar, honey or maple syrup.
6. For a saltish version you can also add 100 ml of either blanched spinach, grated carrot or potato.

Berries

We have to thank the light summer nights of the Northern Hemisphere for the Finnish berry yield.

In good years, nature grows billions of forest berries that are packed with midnight aromas, vitamins, minerals, protective nutrients and fibers. Cultivated berries also develop a particularly strong aroma during those stunning Finnish summer nights.

The forests grow the berries for us for free. All we have to do is to pick them. It would be a shame to leave them there in the woods. It would almost be like leaving 40 million kilos of carrots to rot in the fields.

Garden-grown *strawberries* get to the marketplace just ahead of the forest berries. Thanks to their sweetness, they, too, are eagerly swallowed up by Finnish consumers. The most treasured berries, however, are those picked from the forests.

The first *bilberries,* or *blueberries,* (Vaccinium myrtillus) begin to ripen in mid-July. In good years the bilberry yield is abundant all over Finland. The aroma and colour of the bilberry lend themselves best to sorbets and coulis. Traditionally, bilberry milk is a great favourite. There's nothing quite so summery as a bowlful of bilberries, sprinkled with sugar and steeped in cold milk. Blueberry is also an age-old medicinal herb. The berries have been used, fresh or dried, for the treatment of all kinds of stomach problems. Blueberry is also believed to improve your eye sight. Bilberry leaf tea helps balance variations in blood sugar and is suitable for diabetics.

The *red whortleberry* or *lingonberry* (Vaccinium vitis-idaea) is Finland's most popular berry. The plants grow in light pine heaths and the berries are ripe at the beginning of September. The berries contain benzoic acid and therefore keep well in the fridge, if crushed. Red whortleberries are very nutritious - a kilo's worth contains as much nutrition as three kilos of tomatoes. They were an important source of vitamin for our Finnish ancestors in the winter, and are still widely used in Finland's food culture. Crushed berries go well with all kinds of meat, liver and cabbage dishes. It gives desserts an appetizing colour and the perfect amount of acidity. Red whortleberry juice is also a refreshing drink with food.

The *cloudberry* (Rubus chamaemorus) is northern Finland's most prestigious and perhaps most famous berry. It does, however contain a lot of seeds and offers the taste buds a unique experience. Cloudberry is probably at its best sieved, and served as coulis, in ice cream, sorbets or liqueurs. Cloudberries are notoriously capricious and their yield is intensely affected by the weather. It only takes one frosty night to wipe out the entire harvest. But when everything goes well the northern hillocks can tantalize you with their golden harvest, virtually taunting you to scoop up the berries by the bucketful. Such elegant abundance understandably lures masses of people from southern Finland to make the pilgrimage to Lapland's cloudberry marshes. Many Lapps derive their living from picking cloudberries, so outsiders are not always appreciated.

Several varieties of *currants* (Ribes) are to be found in Finland. Sometimes referred to as Finnish 'grapes', they are used for making home-made wine as well as the official variety. Finnish berry wines are suitable for flavouring sauces and desserts. But they're also brave and tasty for friendly get-togethers and offer an excellent base for summer punches.

The most aromatic of Finnish liqueurs are produced from forest berries. The selection is impressive. *Cranberry* (Vaccinium oxycoccus), *sea buckthorn* (Hippophae rhamnoides), *arctic bramble* (Rubus arcticus), *rowanberry* (Sorbus aucuparia), *wild strawberry* (Fragaria vesca) and *wild raspberry* (Rubus idaeus) are fine for making juices and liqueurs.

Gooseberry Parfait with Caramel Sauce

4 egg yolks
150 ml caster sugar
200 ml gooseberry juice
2 tbsp citrus liqueur
200 ml whipping cream

Sauce:
300 ml caster sugar
300 ml boiling water
50 ml cognac

1. Bring the gooseberry juice to the boil.
2. Whisk the egg yolks with the sugar and add the hot juice, stirring continuously.
3. Return the mixture into a heavy saucepan and allow to thicken over a low heat.
4. Leave to cool. Fold the liqueur and whipped cream into the cool mixture. Pour the mixture into a large mold or into individual serving dishes.
5. Freeze overnight. Unmold the parfait 5-10 minutes before serving and let it stand at room temperature for a while.
6. Prepare the sauce. Melt the sugar in a saucepan and cook until slightly brown. Be careful not to burn it.

7. Allow the sugar to cool down a bit, then pour in the cognac. Light the cognac (not under a cooker hood!).
8. Gradually add boiling water, stirring occasionally. You can substitute part of the water with juice.
9. Cook until slightly reduced. Serve warm.

Midnight Sun Berry Ice Cream

Ice cream mixture for three different ice creams:

1 litre single cream or 500 ml cream and 500 ml milk

12 egg yolks

300-400 ml caster sugar

20 ml alcohol, e.g Koskenkorva or berry liqueur (you can omit the alcohol if you make the ice cream in an ice cream maker)

For the ice creams:

100 ml strawberry purée, sieved
100 ml bilberry purée, sieved
100 ml cloudberry purée, sieved

a sponge cake made with 2 eggs (p. 89)

To glaze:
3 egg whites
4 tbsp icing sugar
50 ml almond flakes

1. Prepare a thin round sponge cake. This will form the cake top.
2. Make the ice cream mixture. Heat the cream in a large saucepan. Mix the egg yolks and sugar together.
3. Pour the hot cream into the egg mixture. Then return it to the saucepan. Stir continuously over gentle heat until thickened.
4. Cool rapidly by immersing the pan in cold water.
5. Divide the ice cream mixture into three and flavour each batch with different berry purées. If desired, you can also add 1 tbsp of a berry liqueur of your choice.
6. Prepare the ice creams in a ice cream maker, one by one, and allow to stand in the freezer.
You can also prepare the ice creams in the freezer. Beat each ice cream occasionally until frozen. Strong alcohol will prevent the ice cream from freezing solid. Omit the alcohol if you're serving the cake to children.
7. Line a 1.5 litre round-bottomed dish with clingfilm and lay the ice creams on its sides in order of readiness so that the last ice cream forms the middle of the cake.

8. Now, lay the sponge cake on top. Moisten with berry liqueur, if desired.
9. Transfer into a freezer until the following day. Cover the cake adequately so as to prevent other tastes being absorbed.
Final touches and serving:
10. Heat the oven to 250°C.
11. Whisk the egg whites and icing sugar until stiff and dry.
12. Turn the cake out onto an ovenproof plate and remove the clingfilm.
13. Spread the meringue carefully all over the cake. Sprinkle with some sugar and almond flakes.
14. Put the cake in the oven and keep an eye on it. Take it out when the meringue has hardened and turned golden-brown.

Pudding Prepared from Honey Made of New Spruce Shoots with Cloudberry coulis

3 egg yolks
1 tbsp caster sugar
3 leaves gelatin; soaked in cold water
50 ml honey made of new spruce shoots*
300 ml whipping cream, whipped

Coulis:
300 ml cloudberry sauce (from strained cloudberries)
2 tbsp caster sugar
50 ml cloudberry liqueur

1. Beat the egg yolks and sugar in a bain-marie until thickened. Add the gelatin, softened in cold water. Leave to cool.
2. Fold in the spruce honey and whipped cream. Spoon into 4 serving dishes and allow to set for 6 hours.
3. Mix the coulis ingredients together and serve with the pudding. Garnish with herb leaves and cloudberries.

*Gather ample amounts of new spruce shoots in the summer. Wash them and immerse them in cold water (just enough to cover them). Bring to the boil. Simmer for 30 minutes. Leave to stand overnight. Strain the milky liquid and add 500 g of sugar for every 1 litre of liquid. Pour into a saucepan and bring to the boil. Simmer, skimming the froth, until the liquid is clear, crimson and syrupy in consistency.

Birch Sap and Melon Soup

500 ml melon, diced (Gallia or green honeydew)
50 ml birch sap
50 ml lemon balm, chopped

100 ml whipping cream, whipped
3 tsp sea buckthorn liqueur

1. Mash the melon and dilute with the birch sap. Add the lemon balm and mix.
2. Serve the soup cold on a deep plate together with the whipped cream, flavoured with the sea buckthorn liqueur.

Strawberry Cheesecake

6 eggs
150 ml caster sugar
200 ml finely ground hazelnuts
75 ml plain flour
50 ml potato flour
1 tsp baking powder

Filling:
8 leaves gelatin, softened in cold water
1 tbsp lemon juice
250 g low-fat curd cheese or quark
500 ml strawberry purée
100 ml caster sugar
200 ml whipping cream, whipped

For moistening:
150 ml orange juice

To decorate:
300 ml whipping cream, whipped
1 tbsp vanilla sugar
caster sugar
500 ml strawberries
50 ml toasted almond flakes
lemon balm leaves

1. Whisk the eggs and sugar together until frothy.
2. Mix the dry ingredients together and add them to the egg mixture, stirring gently.
3. Pour the mixture into a greased, 24-cm loose-bottom cake tin.
4. Bake in a 200°C oven for 30-40 minutes.
5. Prepare the filling. Dissolve the softened gelatins in hot lemon juice. Allow to cool.
6. Mix the strawberry purée and sugar with the low-fat curd cheese or quark until smooth.
7. Add the dissolved gelatin and, finally, fold in the whipped cream.
8. Leave to set for a moment in the fridge.
9. Divide the cake into three parts.
10. Line a cake tin with clingfilm. Lay a layer of cake in the bottom of the tin. Moisten with orange juice and spread the filling on top. Repeat and, if desired, finish off with some filling.
11. Cover the cake well with clingfilm and allow to set in a cool place until the following day.
12. Turn the cake out onto a serving plate and decorate with whipped cream, strawberries and lemon balm leaves.

Bilberry pie is definitely a staple of Finnish baking tradition. The first bilberries are usually ripe during the last week of July. This is known as "women's week" in Finland since all the name days in that week are female. Bilberry pies are therefore considered a suitably celebratory dish. Recipes for bilberry pies abound. Some believe that only a yeast dough can give rise to a genuine bilberry pie. Others, however, favour short crust pastry. Thanks to age-old traditions, either approach guarantees delicious results.

Berry Tartlets

Pastry:
150 g butter
50 ml caster sugar
1 egg
350 ml plain flour

Patisserie:
200 ml whipping cream
250 ml milk
1 vanilla pod, split
5 egg yolks
3 1/2 tbsp cornflour
4 tbsp caster sugar

Jelly:
100 ml red berry juice or syrup
1 leaf gelatin, softened in cold water

500 ml fresh berries (strawberries, raspberries, bilberries and cloudberries)

1. Prepare the tartlets. Cream the butter and sugar together.
2. Add the egg and flour. Mix until smooth.
3. Shape the pastry into a roll. Cut into pieces and press them into greased tart tins.
4. Bake in a 200°C oven for about 15 minutes. Cool on a wire rack.
5. Prepare the patisserie. Place the milk, cream and vanilla pod in a saucepan. Bring to the boil.
6. Stir the egg yolks with a fork. Add the sugar, mixed with the cornflour.
7. Pour on the hot cream and milk mixture, stirring continuously. Then return to the saucepan.
8. Heat in a double saucepan until thick.
9. Leave to cool, stirring at times. Remove the vanilla pod and pour the prepared cream into a piping bag.
10. Dissolve the softened gelatin in some juice. Add the rest of the juice.
11. Pipe the cream into the tartlets. Arrange a layer of fresh berries on top.
12. Brush the berries with the jelly.

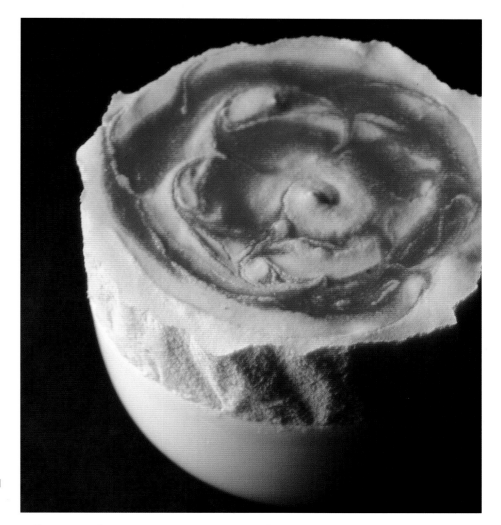

Cold Arctic Bramble Soufflé

4 egg yolks
50 ml caster sugar
50 ml arctic bramble liqueur
7-8 leaves gelatin, softened in cold water
250 ml arctic bramble purée
500 ml whipping cream, whipped
4 egg whites
100 ml icing sugar

1. Beat the egg yolks lightly. Stir in the sugar and liqueur.
2. Thicken the mixture in a bain-marie.
3. Stir in the softened gelatin. Allow to cool.
4. Whisk the egg whites and sugar until soft peaks form.
5. Carefully fold the arctic bramble purée and whipped cream into the cool egg yolk mixture.
6. Finally, fold in the whisked egg whites.
7. Line small ramekins with foil, so that the foil comes about 2 cm above the edges. This will enable the soufflés to reach a greater height.
8. Spoon the soufflé mixture into the prepared ramekins.
9. Leave to set in the fridge for 24 hours.
10. Remove the foil edge before serving and dust with icing sugar.

Christmas Menu

Clear Trumpet Chanterelle soup

(makes about 2 litres)

300 g carrots
50 g leek
a small piece of parsnip
a small piece of celeriac
500 ml fresh or frozen trumpet
chanterelles
200 g onions, chopped
oil or butter for frying
4 litres water
1 tbsp fine sea salt
thyme (fresh or dried)
rosemary (fresh or dried)
5 whole black peppers

1. Clean the vegetables and cut them into slices about 1 cm thick.
2. Toast them in a hot, dry frying pan until golden brown. Set aside.
3. Sweat the mushrooms and onions in butter or oil. Leave some for garnish.
4. Put the toasted vegetables into a saucepan with the cold water and add part of the mushroom and onion mixture.
5. Start cooking the broth. Skim off any foam. When the foam stops forming, add the seasoning.
6. Simmer for 2 hours.
7. Strain the broth. Add the rest of the sweated mushrooms and onion in the soup before serving.
8. Serve hot, with mushroom tartlets.

Mushroom Tartlets

Pastry:
100 g butter
250-300 ml plain flour
a pinch of salt
2 tbsp water

Filling:
1 tbsp butter
500 ml chopped mushrooms (1 litre fresh mushrooms)
100 ml chopped leek
100 ml sour cream
50 ml chopped herbs (basil and parsley)
salt and freshly ground black pepper
150 ml grated Black label Emmenthal

1. Prepare the pastry. Put the butter, flour and salt into a mixing bowl. Rub the fat into flour until the mixture is crumbly. Add the water and mix briefly until smooth.
2. Shape the dough into a roll and leave in the fridge for 30 minutes.
3. In the meanwhile, prepare the filling. Sweat the mushrooms and leek in butter. Add the sour cream and simmer for 5 minutes.
4. Season the filling with herbs, pepper and salt. Add half of the grated cheese. Leave to cool.
5. Remove the pastry from the fridge. Cut into 15 pieces and press into greased tart tins.
6. Spoon in the filling and sprinkle with the rest of the grated cheese.
7. Bake in a 200°C oven for 20-30 minutes, depending on the size of the tins.
8. Leave to cool for a moment. Then remove from the tins.

Christmas Menu

Roast Christmas Ham

1 slightly salted gammon

Glazing:
3 tbsp mustard
1 tbsp golden syrup or honey
1 tbsp potato flour
1 egg yolk
3 tbsp breadcrumbs

Sauce:
500 ml pan juices, skimmed
2 tbsp cornflour
100 ml whipping cream
100 ml apple sauce
honey
cinnamon
lemon juice

Melt the frozen ham carefully in a cool place for 1-5 days, depending on the size. A gammon containing a bone takes a longer time than a boneless one. The gammon must be at room temperature before being put into the oven. Check with a meat thermometer! Put the gammon in a roasting tin, rindside up and insert the meat thermometer into the gammon's thickest point so that the tip of it doesn't touch the bone. Pour about 100 ml of water into the tin. The ham should become succulent if you roast it in a 90-120°C oven. The ham is ready when the meter indicates 77-80°C. Roasting time varies from 1 to 2 hours per kilo of meat. Let the ham rest for a while before cutting off the rind.

Sauce:
Preserve the pan juices, strain and, after cooling, prepare a sauce from the liquid. It's then easy to skim the extra fat off the surface. Season the liquid with honey and a dash of lemon juice. Add some apple juice, a little cinnamon and the cornflour. Simmer for 5 minutes. If desired, add 100 ml whipping cream.

Glazing the ham:
Put the ham in an ovenproof dish. Mix the mustard, syrup or honey, potato flour and egg yolk until smooth. Spread the mixture on top of the ham and sprinkle with breadcrumbs. Gratinate in a 200-225°C oven until nicely browned.

Beetroot-marinated Salmon

600 g boneless salmon fillet
3 tbsp coarse sea salt
freshly ground black pepper
200 g grated fresh beetroot
1 tbsp grated horseradish
50 ml oil
20 ml Koskenkorva (or Finlandia vodka)

Beetroot sauce:
200 ml cooked beetroot, mashed
1 tsp Dijon mustard
1 tbsp sugar
4 tbsp red wine vinegar
100 ml oil
a pinch of salt
freshly ground black pepper

1. Marinate the salmon in the salt for 24 hours. (see page 18)
2. Mix the grated vegetables together and add the oil and alcohol.
3. Spread the mixture evenly on the fish and marinate in the fridge for one more day.
4. Prepare the sauce. Mix the mashed beetroot, mustard and sugar in a blender.
5. Add the vinegar and oil, alternately.
6. Season with salt and pepper.
7. Wipe the vegetable mixture off the salmon and cut into thin slices. Arrange them on a plate and pour sauce around them.

Christmas Menu

Traditional Potato Casserole

1.3 kg floury potatoes
water
50 g butter
1 1/2 tbsp plain flour
300-400 ml milk
1 1/2 tsp salt

1. Scrub the potatoes and boil them in unsalted water until done. Peel them while hot and mash them together with the butter. Allow to cool.
2. Stir 1/2 tbsp flour into the mash. Allow to stand, covered, for a few hours at room temperature. Add the rest of the flour intermittently into the mash, mixing well.
3. Add enough milk to make a loose mash. Season with salt. Pour the mixture into either a single greased 2-litre ovenproof dish or two smaller ones. Leave enough room on the sides.
4. Bake in a 150°C oven for about 3 hours.

Swede Casserole

1.3 kilos swede, peeled and diced
water and salt
100 ml breadcrumbs
150 ml whipping cream
2 eggs
1/2 tsp ground ginger
1/4 tsp ground white pepper
1/4 tsp ground nutmeg
2 tbsp golden syrup
butter
breadcrumbs

1. Boil the swede in salted water until done. Save some of the cooking water.
2. Mash the swede either with a hand mixer or in a blender.
3. Mix the breadcrumbs with the cream. Allow to stand to swell.
4. Add about 200 ml of cooking water into the mashed swede. Then add the soaked breadcrumbs together with the eggs, seasoning and syrup.
5. Grease a 2-litre ovenproof dish or two smaller ones and spoon the swede mixture into it.
6. Sprinkle with breadcrumbs and bake in a 200°C oven for about 1 hour.

Ginger Snap Parfait with Strawberry Purée

500 ml whipping cream
200 ml hot milk
150 ml sugar
6 egg yolks
12 ginger snaps, crushed
strawberries, puréed and sweetened

1. Mix the egg yolks and sugar together in a saucepan.
2. Pour the hot milk into the mixture.
3. Stir continuously over heat until thickened.
4. Add the crushed ginger snaps and let them melt in the mixture.
5. Allow to cool. Add the lightly whipped cream and mix until smooth.
6. Pour into a parfait mould or other freezer-proof dish and freeze overnight.
7. Bring the parfait to room temperature 30 minutes before serving. Serve with strawberry purée.

The Finnish Language

Though sparsely-populated and modest on the world map, Finland still boasts its own language - *suomi*.

Known in English as Finnish, it's distantly related to Hungarian. The language wasn't officially recognized until the 19th century, and yet the oldest Finnish words date back 5,000 years or more to the Finno-Ugric and Uralian period. Words that refer to relatives, such as *emä* (mother); *isä* (father); *lapsi* (child); *appi* (father-in-law); and *anoppi* (mother-in-law) are among the oldest. Perhaps one of the reasons why foreigners consider Finnish so difficult is because of its versatility. Its syntax is extremely flexible, giving rise to endless nuances. Standard colloquial Finnish is freely mixed with a variety of dialects, slang and words from other languages. In fact, Finnish is so versatile that it's even possible to construct new words for specific or new situations.

As in most countries, Finland enjoys many colourful, local dialects. Many families also employ their very own vocabulary or particular linguistic style. So, in Finland, we can even think of there being family or individual dialects. The Finnish language is also extremely onomatopoeic. The actual resonance of the words enable the speaker to relate his message accurately and vividly.

Finns love their language. Millions of books are printed in Finnish every year. And books are still the most popular gifts for special occasions, including Christmas and birthdays. According to research, ten-year-old Finnish children are the most literate of their age in the whole world.

Finns also believe in and exert the power of the spoken word. They are avid theatre-goers and Finnish amateur dramatics enjoys nation-wide enthusiasm.

The Finnish national epic, the *Kalevala*, has been translated into several languages, as have Mika Waltari's 'Sinuhe the Egyptian', Väinö Linna's 'The Unknown Soldier', Tove Jansson's 'Moomin' books, etc.

Despite - or perhaps because of - its obscureness, the Finnish language definitely holds a certain allure, at least among academics. At present, it's taught in over 70 universities in various parts of the world.

The Whooper Swan (Cygnus cygnus) The swan was voted Finland's national bird in 1981. Karelians have long held it as holy; symbolizing purity, light and beauty. It also has a pertinent role in the Finnish national epic, the Kalevala.

Wood Anemone (Anemone nemorosa) Wood anemones proclaim the Finnish spring with a prolific floral display. They're also often given to mums on the second Sunday in May, Mother's Day in Finland.

The Sauna

The sauna is a constant and beloved institution in Finland. It has helped shape Finland's history and can even affect the economy of the country.

Traditionally, the sauna has not only been a place for washing; a wide range of important tasks and activities have also taken place there. Saunas have been used as breweries, curehouses and laundries.

Sauna dressing rooms have been used as living-quarters for farm hands and sons-in-law. Political outcasts hid in saunas. In the wilds the sauna provided crucial hiding places during the wars. The story also goes that, in the war years, Finnish soldiers frequently had saunas in order to regain their strength for the struggle against the Russians. Historical fact certainly records that saunas were built all the way up to the front lines.

Many an elderly Finn was born in a sauna. It's been the place to treat illness, give massages and go about that very Finnish tradition of cupping bad blood.

In all probability, there's not a single Finn in the world who has never had a sauna.

Saunas can be found high and low, even if Finland is basically flat. And Finns derive extraordinary delight from having a sauna in a location which is as remote and unlikely as possible. It's not unusual for an executive in Helsinki to assert that the best saunas can only be found in Lapland and, in a whim, resolve to travel there. The distance is roughly the same as from London to Barcelona. But as soon as this modern citizen sits on the top bench of the sauna and throws the very first ladle of water onto the sizzling stones he knows that the trek has been well worthwhile.

The sauna is not essentially erotic. It's at its best when you're there alone. The sauna can offer you a tour of your inner self. It's a haven for feeling and listening to the basics of life. No sooner have you started chopping wood for the sauna than you notice an inner calm; you are astute. The dry wood gives off a strong smell and cuts easily under your axe. Each blow expels pent-up frustrations. The fire in the sauna burns off any remaining anxieties.

Hot stones, steam, hot air: it relieves stress and anxiety. Whisking the body softens your muscles even more. The aroma from the birch leaves brings with it an almost spiritual calmness. Water rinses away all that's old. In the sauna Finns are born again.

The Rowan

Sorbus aucuparia

'"Sour," said the fox of the rowanberry.'

It's estimated that the rowan came to Finland over 7,000 years ago. It has always been a popular tree for the yard since it's thought to protect the garden from evil spirits. In the *Kalevala*, the Finnish national epic, the rowan was a holy tree, dedicated to the spouse of the Almighty. It protected nature from His raging furies: lightning. Its branches were also believed to hold magic powers for hunters. The Almighty left alone all those who had cut off a rowan branch and slept with it.

Rowan has also been chosen as the most beautiful tree in Finland. In the spring its white flowers blossom, pervading the air with their sweet smell and attracting insects. In the summer it's lusciously green and shields the garden from even the fiercest of winds. In the autumn its branches bend under the weight of its scarlet berries and its leaves turn crimson red. The amount of flowers and berries has also acted as an omen for the forthcoming winter.

An old saying goes:
The more the blossom, the less the snow.
Two loads the rowan surely will not show

Rowan leaves are good for fodder and tea, its bark for dyeing. The wood of the rowan is excellent for making furniture. A bittersweet jam can be made from rowanberries, which goes perfectly with game. Rowanberries are also used for making wine, liqueur and sweets.

The Norway Spruce

Picea abies

'*Listen to the spruce nearest your home.*' - A Finnish adage

The spruce's potency in Finnish culture is verified by its unassailable position in the forest. It's valuable as building timber and for the paper industry. It also provides the raw material for fine paper and viscose.

Spruce branches, cones and shoots are used extensively as decoration. Spruces can surround a house and provide a solid, natural fence. Spruce branches are used to cover plants to help protect them from winter. They're laid out on steps for people to wipe their feet on. In days gone by, the branches were made into brooms for sweeping the snow off garden paths.

As a fully-decorated Christmas tree it can even perpetuate the ideals of the tree of life.

In spring, its new bright-green shoots are vibrant and packed with vitamins. The shoots can be used to revitalize salads. You can make marmalade from them.

Spruce branches have been added to bath water for the relief of colds and rheumatism.

A spruce forest is sublime. The moss carpet is usually at its thickest there. It's also a haven for mushrooms, not to mention mushroom-pickers.

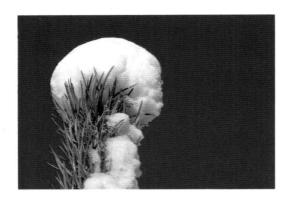

The Scots Pine

Pinus silvestris

It's the sturdy Scots pine which best captures the essence of the Finnish character.

Many a Finn would wish to be as solid and trustworthy as a Scots pine tree

On the other hand, perhaps the Scots pine is a wee bit too serious.

In all probability, the pine is Finland's most photographed and painted tree. Bathed in the evening sun, its trunk becomes reddish and golden.

Wood processing is a major industry in Finland. Pine is an abundant timber species here and a much-valued material for house building, interior decorating and the furniture industry.

Pine oil and pine soap are by-products of the pulp-making process.

An original Finnish custom of washing rugs in the summertime is to make practical use of the nearest lake or stretch of sea. The combination of pine soap and sea water or fresh water gives the carpets a remarkably fresh and clean smell. Pine soap does not pollute the environment and is ideally suited to the treatment of wooden floors. In fact, it can even offer you a painless means of cleaning your dog's fur.

A few drops of essential pine oil is all it takes to give a room that really fresh smell. The air is exceptionally clean and healthy in the midst of a pine forest. No wonder Finns go there to relax and recuperate.

Pine smells good. It makes for non-crackling firewood, perfect for fireplaces and open fires. Finns hold pine so dearly that it's also the most-favoured wood for building summer cottages and saunas with. Lapland's grey, dead standing pine is a popular and 'primitive' building material for lodges in the wilds.

Pine needles smell of resin. Their aroma has established them as a herb. The needles are able to withstand the winter temperatures extremely well. They can thaw and freeze over, time and time again, without coming apart.

Even in the depths of winter pine trees offer a reassuring greenness to the Finnish landscape. They provide basic nutrition for elks, wood grouse and a vast variety of small forest animals. Their roots give host to delicious mushrooms such as false morel.

The Weeping Birch and The Silver Birch

Betula pubescens and Betula pendula

The birch cheers everyone up. It's beautiful at any time of year. In winter it wears a gently-frosted mantle. In summer it dons a cool and composed green cape. In autumn it sports a red and yellow gown. But it's the birch's summer outfit - featuring a white trunk and green leaves - that captures the senses. A birch in bloom has long been regarded as a symbol of joy and new life. Some believe that the birch actually holds such magical properties right up until Midsummer and perhaps beyond. Finns decorate their doorways with birch at midsummer.

Understandably, birch leaves are defiantly attached to their branches at this time. It's the best time to make sauna whisks for the winter. A birch whisk made during midsummer brings more than a residue of summer to the remoteness of winter. Birch wood also offers the most constant and intense heat for the sauna stove.

It takes the warmth of the late spring sun to activate the vitality of the birch. That's when water starts to rush throughout the trunk towards the top and branches. You can even try to milk its sap if you have the patience. Birch sap tastes sweet and contains a lot of vitamins and minerals. Birch's sugar, xylitol, is used as a sweetening agent in sweets and chewing gum. It's far better for teeth than ordinary sugar. The tree's young leaves are good for tea and salads, as well as offering a delicious edge to soups. Birch leaf tea acts as a diuretic.

Birch also guarantees forest-owners top prices. Printing paper made from birch produces an attractive, shiny white surface. Birch wood is also used in the manufacture of exquisite light furniture and plywood.

The tough and tight characteristics of birch bark made it the forerunner of plastic and rubber in Finland. It used to be the most popular material for constructing waterproof roofs. Herdsmen used it for making shoes, carry-cases and lunch-boxes. They made string from it. It could be made into cups for scooping water out of chilly streams or gathering juicy berries. Even today, the extraordinary Finnish Easter pudding, *mämmi*, is usually packed in a cardboard box printed in bark relief.

Birch is also an important tree for animals. Birds use it as their nesting tree and a place for song. Elk, deer and reindeer relish young birch leaves.

Ostrich Fern

(Matteuccia struthinopteris) The ostrich fern adds a flourish to luscious groves and the banks of streams.

Witch's Hair Lichen

(Usnea hirta) Witch's hair lichen needs an extremely clean climate in order to thrive. It can still be found in Finland's virgin forests.

Mosses and Lichen

Green mosses cover shadowy stones and the lowermost parts of the forest. They feel squishy underfoot.
Lichen grows on the forest floor, over rocks or on tree trunks. It grows extremely slowly, but withstands aridness and extreme temperature changes.

Lily of the Valley

(Convallaria majalis) Lily of the valley was voted Finland's national flower in 1967. Its heady scent starts to permeate the undergrowth at the beginning of June. Its petite bell-shaped flowers gently rouse romantic notions in us. Lily of the valley is also a very popular choice for bridal bouquets as well as an early declaration of summer for the home.

Convallaria majalis is Latin for lily of the valley and eludes directly to the Old Testament. Lily of the valley has been viewed as the flower of paradise as well a symbol of the Virgin Mary and the Second Coming of Christ. Hence, perhaps, its popularity as a Christmas flower.

Chickweed Wintergreen

(Trienalis europaea) Chickweed wintergreen grows all over Finland and delights the forest visitor with its small, delicate flower.

(Oxeye) Daisy

(Leucanthemum vulgare) Daisies are an inseparable part of the Finnish landscape.

Spectrolite

is a unique semiprecious stone only found in Finland. It has various applications and is highly popular for making stylish watches and clocks. Spectrolite derives its name from the ever-changing hues of blues and greens that sparkle on its surface.

Granite

represents the rock-solid basis of Finnish terrain. Its colour range spans from pale-and dark-grey to reddish-grey, giving a rugged and hearty appearance to public buildings and expansive surfaces in flat rock. Granite is also used for making jewelry and ornaments.Huge amounts of it were used as the construction material for the official residence of Finland's President.

Rosebay Willowherb or Fireweed

(Epilobum angustifolium) At the end of the summer rosebay willowherb fills all the headlands with its purple flowers. In Finland it's also known as the 'rotter's rose', in reference to it being an improvident gift for a wife from a husband returning after a night on the town. Its young spring shoots can be used in much the same way as lettuce, spinach or asparagus.

Nettle

(Urtica dioica)Everyone knows the nettle. It's avoided and belittled but it is, in fact, an age-old medicinal herb and the most nutritious and healthy of all vegetable plants. Creamed nettles go well with fish dishes. Nettle soup is really delicious and dried nettles can be used to brew tea and flavour bread doughs. Nettle gives wool a beautiful green colour.

Cornflower

(Centaurea cyanus) The cornflower is a symbol of earthly happiness and heavenly love. Since it's blue, it's also thought of as a very Finnish flower.

Waxwing

(Bombycilla garrulus) Waxwings chirping in the rowans is a familiar and much-welcomed sight and sound for many Finns. Whilst eating rowanberries, they also often snap up fermented berries. The waxwing's metabolism, however, has adapted well to the demands of burning off alcohol. Nevertheless, it's not unusual to spot tipsy waxwings wandering around aimlessly with smiles on their faces. Fortunately, recovery-time is short.

Birds

The majority of Finland's fifty million nesting birds migrate for winter. Nevertheless, no less than twenty million daring individuals brave the trials of winter and stay put. Thirty-three endangered species nest in Finland. These include the lesser white-fronted eagle, the white-tailed eagle and the corncrake, all of which are under a genuine threat of extinction.

Capercaillie

also known as Wood Grouse (Tetrao urogallus). 'Fighting capercaillies', a painting by Ferdinand von Wright, is familiar to all Finns. The mating call of wood grouse cocks, their fights, the unmistakable rustling of their wings, reflect the innermost qualities of the northern wilderness: strength and endurance.

Dipper

(Cinclus cinclus) The dipper is the only bird that migrates in large numbers to Finland for the winter. It also happens to be the only passerine species that obtains its food by diving into water.

Black Woodpecker

(Dryocopus martius) Akseli Gallen-Kallela, a famous Finnish painter, celebrated the black woodpecker in many of his paintings. Until then the bird was generally considered to be a bad omen, auguring bad weather or disaster. It has a piercing sound and brings vitality to an otherwise unperturbed winter forest.

Golden Eagle

(Aquila chrysaetos) The golden eagle, the king of birds, has been a symbol of power and glory for centuries. The role of the eagle is of paramount importance in the Finnish national epic, the Kalevala. It's said that the bonfires that burn on Midsummer Night's Eve are a sacrificial flame for the thunder bird, the progenitor of the Finnish tribe.

Summer

June

Summer is the season most longed for in Finland. Spring brings forth light but only summer can release the sun's energy. The Finnish names for the summer months reveal the precise character of each 'moon'. Kesäkuu, the summer month, signals the advent of summer. Heinäkuu, the hay month, refers to the gathering of hay for winter fodder. Elokuu, the crop month, tells us that the crops are ripening, harvest time is upon us. The weather at the beginning of June can be very changeable. Some years summer comes early, within the first few weeks of June. Other years summertime can be tantalizingly late. The forest berries also flower in early summer. Finns remain ever hopeful that the weather will stay warm so frosts won't ruin their gardens or kill off blossoming wild berries. Bathed in the warmth of the sun, nature explodes into a lush, green spectacle. Conifers join in the celebration, adorned in endless hues of emerald leaves, bordered by forest meadows and headlands that vibrate with abundant varieties of deciduous trees and wild flowers. The interaction of continuous light and warmth generates a frenzied period of growth. Such is its impact that Finland's short summer can yield practically all the nutrition needed to sustain its inhabitants; animal or human. Fish spawn in the lakes and the sea. Birds are still nesting in the woods. As soon as the meadows turn green the cows are driven to pasture. This can be a rather comical procedure. After many monotonous months in the cow-shed the cows run and jump along the green meadows to their hearts' content. Fresh grass fortifies the milk. The cows can be outside for the whole of the summer. They can find more than enough shade in the trees, even under the sweltering midsummer sun.

People put away their mittens, woolly hats and other winter gear. No one even wants to catch a glimpse of them during the summer months.

Midsummer - The Highlight of the Finnish Summer

Early June is filled with expectation. We're looking forward to Midsummer, the most important and revered celebration of the Finnish summer. Exactly six months have passed since the darkest day of the year. Now it's time to celebrate the longest and lightest day of the year. In southern Finland the sun dips briefly beyond the horizon, in northern Finland it doesn't set at all.

Bonfires burn ceremoniously on the shores of tens of thousands of lakes. Homes are meticulously swept and cleaned. Birch trees and blossoming rowan branches adorn front doors and porches. Lilacs in bloom and midsummer roses are arranged in vases. You can even see cars decorated with birch leaves in the countryside.

Finnish towns are virtually deserted. Finns wind their way to their cottages in search of birches and a suitable lake-side location for their Midsummer bonfires.

If the early summer has been hot and dry it may be too dangerous to run the risk of open fires. In which case people simply go to the sauna, drink beer, grill sausages, pop open bottles of sparkling wine or unscrew the tops of something a little stronger.

In short, Finns let the long-awaited summer seep in, thereby distancing themselves from the harsh realities of winter.

The Finnish flag flies at full mast throughout the night. On Midsummer's Day people get together for a Midsummer lunch. At long last the kitchen is able to offer new potatoes and dill, slightly salted salmon and whitefish, Baltic herring and herring served in a variety of ways. Rhubarb fool and whipped cream complete the feast. Many couples want to be married at Midsummer so church bells are ringing. Meanwhile, the cynics are muttering: "That's the end of summer, then. Now the days are pulling in again."

Birch is synonymous with June. Its colour changes from psychedelic green to darker hues as the leaves gain their full size. The leaves cling tightly to the branches. That's why sauna whisks made during midsummer don't lose their leaves even in the depths of winter.

Rowans are blooming and give out a powerful perfume. Blossoming white and blue lilacs also give off a heady bouquet.

Mosquitoes pester people in the evenings. Perhaps the Finnish summer would be too perfect without them. Fortunately, their whimpering gives us fair warning. They fly lethargically and are easy to snuff out. There are plenty of sprays and deterrents on the market. As regards their prey, mosquitoes have a liking for some more than others. The reason is unclear. There is a belief that if you drink enough beer they won't come near you.

One thing's for sure: if you drink enough you probably won't notice them. Finns have learnt to live with mosquitoes. After all, they have their part to play in the food chain; they're the staple diet of our precious swallows.

July

July is the most popular holiday month in Finland. Finns are at their summer cottages. Ideally, the cottage should be situated in a secluded and quiet setting since Finns see their vacation as an opportunity to reflect, rest and escape from the trials of winter, without the intrusion of others. The cottages aren't necessarily luxurious. Finns often feel the need to 'return to nature' on holiday. A busy executive knows no better way to meditate than by chopping wood and fetching buckets of water for the sauna tubs. Modern technology, however, is creeping into the cottage kitchen. The idea being to minimize household chores in the pursuit of a romantic country life. Fishing from your own shore is another 'must' for a Finn on holiday. Children use a hook-and-line to catch small

perch. Traps and nets yield bigger fish for soups and grander dishes. Summer mornings are often beautifully still in Finland. To many Finns, the brim of a sunrise, when the dew of the night still lingers over the surface of the water, can be summer's most breathtaking moment. The birds are up, holding a dawn chorus in the leafy groves of the shore. The oars of the wooden boat squeak melodiously with each pull. At around four or five in the morning the fish bites best around the edge of the rushes. It's breakfast time: the pike is there waiting for small fish, the fisherman's hook is there waiting for the pike. A Finn's cottage provides a sanctuary after the humdrum of the working day. Sitting alone on the sauna steps or on a rock by the shore is good for your soul. No obligations, no need to socialize, no need to do anything. You can feel free, relax and recharge yourself, ready for the rigours of working life.

Finns want to eat as simply as possible in the summer. The basic ingredients are so good that barely anything needs to be done to them. New potatoes are quickly boiled in

salted water and amply seasoned with strong-scented summer dill. There's a wide selection of fish and plenty of ways of preparing them; grilled, smoked, slightly salted or flame-baked. A small knob of butter suffices as a sauce. Fresh tomatoes and cucumber make up the salad. Only rye bread is served as an extra. People prefer to cook and eat outside as often as possible. In the evenings, for larger appetites, it's a time for grilling marinated steaks, cutlets and sausages. During the hottest time of the day a jar of *viili* and a sandwich are enough to abate your hunger. And, even in the summer, guests are steadfastly served coffee, together with berry tart or cake. In addition to new potatoes, July also brings strawberries to the market place. Thanks to the midnight sun, they're succulent and sweet and quickly devoured. They're at their best *au naturel*, but you are allowed to enhance them with whipped cream and some vanilla sugar. Strawberry cakes, together with a sprinkling of strawberry parties and festivals are also an integral part of the Finnish summer.

If Finns aren't taking it easy at their own cottages they're travelling around, visiting relatives or attending some of the country's numerous summer festivals. They're sailing off the shores of southern Finland or dancing tango in western Finland. They're listening to opera and classical music in eastern Finland and panning for gold in the north. There are hundreds of events, big and small, all over the country.

August

August must bid a reluctant and tender farewell to even the most gorgeous of summers. The evenings become progressively darker and cooler. Walking along a familiar summery path you are suddenly aware of the odours of an approaching autumn. If the summer has been hot and dry the first birches are already beginning to turn bright yellow. The birds' concerto has faded to little more than a few chirps. Their routine has been replaced by grasshoppers who start their evening performance just as soon as the dusk settles. The evenings are so dark the full moon shines down in almost winter brilliance.

People return to the towns: work begins, school starts. Yet the evenings are still warm. The crayfish season gets underway. School children can earn some hefty pocket money by catching crayfish for restaurants and gourmets.

Finnish crayfish are extremely expensive, so only the most affluent can afford to buy them for August's crayfish parties. Some people, however, just happen to have their cottage right next to a crayfish-rich lake. These fortunate individuals get to enjoy such spoils for free. Catching crayfish is not particularly easy and it's only possible at night. But it is fun. The crayfish are cooked in salted water which is rapidly brought to the boil and seasoned with flowering dill. The herb smells and tastes pungently of caraway, an ideal garnish for crayfish.

Drinking songs are the hallmark of Finnish-Swedish tradition during crayfish parties. But anyone can join in, even those who *can* sing in tune.

Crayfish are best washed down with water and beer. The optional snaps must be perfectly chilled. If it's too warm it can obscure the taste and thus inhibit the crayfish's delicate aroma. That's why some of us skip the snaps and opt for dry white wine or a more sparkling variety.

Those who can't afford crayfish may grill a large catch of perch instead, and eat them crayfish-style. Some may even simply boil a pan of garden peas. The diners are dutifully equipped with snaps glasses, filled with

melted butter, which they hold in front of them. The thoroughly-cooked pea pods are then ceremoniously dipped into the melted butter and the peas drawn into the mouth with the help of one's teeth.

August witnesses summer's ample harvest in the market places. Bilberries ripen and are

picked for bilberry milk shakes and pies. A good 'blueberry' year can yield around 90 million kilos of bilberries in the Finnish forests.

The first mushrooms, chanterelles and ceps, also appear in the woods. Summer's harvest festival, autumn, has arrived.

Autumn

Autumn is viewed as winter's waiting room in Finland. Finns also say that autumn 'is driven by nine horses', meaning that it's climatically changeable. One moment it's raining, the next it's sunny. Storms and tranquility share equal footing. The days pull in, in leaps and bounds. Daylight diminishes, nighttime invades.

At the latitude of Helsinki, after the autumnal equinox on September the 23rd, every day is six minutes shorter than the previous one. In northern Finland the process is even more dramatic. The deciduous birch and maple gradually begin to draw chlorophyll into their buds and branches for the oncoming winter. If the nights are frosty the rowan and aspen leaves explode into an array of bright red. The yellowness of the leaves contrasts strikingly with the azure of the sky, startling even the most casual of observers. Finnish forests glow with autumnal hues. The most spectacular displays are to be found in Lapland, where the frost has managed to paint the leaves red before they dry up and an autumn storm has had time to tear them off. Leaves are dried for household decoration,

dried hay is arranged in vases. Finns rake their gardens and yards. The forest smells of moss and mushrooms invade the air. Mosquitoes have gone into hibernation. It's invigorating to amble around an autumnal forest. There's nowhere coffee tastes better than in the woods, poured out of a thermos, particularly if you're sitting intrepidly on a tree stump.

Finns love rambling in mushroom forests. Three million Finns gather berries or mushrooms every year. In the early autumn it's a time for chanterelles, ceps and russula. Later on it's the turn of milk caps. Towards the end of autumn, right up until the frosts win out, trumpet chanterelles provide easy pickings. Most of the birds have already flown south. The last migrants; starlings, chaffinches and skylarks, sit atop telephone wires in long rows, waiting for the appropriate wind to migrate on. The swans are the last to go. Waxwings stay in Finland as long as there are rowanberries in the trees.

Tables on market places bend under the weight of onions, vegetables, potatoes and other root vegetables. It's the time of preserves. Cellars are filled with jams, juices and pickles. Reluctantly, cows return to their sheds.

The animals are plump. They've eaten themselves silly in anticipation of the winter.

It's the peak of the hunting season. 300,000 Finnish men hunt. Their quarry include elk and wild reindeer. It's time to round up reindeer in the north. Forest birds such as doves, wild duck, willow grouse, wood grouse and black grouse are also caught. Lambs are led to the slaughter.

In autumn, fat whitefish and salmons are hauled in from the sea. Salmon is at its cheapest. The shiny-sided Baltic herring even has an autumn festival held in its honour.

The diminishing light affects Finns in much the same way it affects the rest of creation. We all need more sleep. We get tired and lethargic easily. Many of us are in low spirits. But for the majority of Finns the darkness, contrasting drastically with the relentless daylight of summer, also triggers a period of inner calm.

October is the busiest month of the year for libraries. Autumn heralds the advent of new hobbies, meditation, language courses and physical fitness classes.

People like to stay at home in autumn. Potatoes, root vegetables and jars of preservatives are stacked in long rows in cellars. Home-made wine bubbles merrily in the kitchen. The Finnish fall lends itself to reading, watching television and going to the theatre.

Electric lights and candles appear in trees and gardens. Candles burn and fireplaces flicker. On the sixth of December, at six o'clock in the evening, candles are lit on window sills to commemorate Finland's Independence Day. That occasion demands restrained celebration: people dress in their finest clothes and eat Finnish food. Game is popular, e.g. roast reindeer or venison. The President hosts a huge ball at the palace, and the entire occasion is broadcast live on TV. Finnish embassies arrange receptions all over the world.

The first Christmas parties are held as early as November. Companies organize parties for their staff. Friends invite each other to their homes. This is how people get into the Christmas spirit. We drink mulled wine, eat a wide selection of pies and taste Christmas pastries filled with plum jam.

Christmas

Many thank God for Christmas time. It delivers us from autumn and proclaims our winter. It's a celebration of light during the darkest time of year. A Finnish Christmas carol declares:

"Well, it seems that summer has arrived [in reference to a Christmas tree] in the midst of winter, so let's make a nest for the little birds...".

Christmas too, of course, has its own tree. And the spruce is a good safe choice. When you look out of the window, there's nothing more reassuring than to see a sturdy spruce standing there, strong and stable. Finns find the spruce extremely masculine. Spruce calms the spirit after those frantic Christmas preparations. Traditionally, it's only brought in on Christmas Eve. By the time the family starts decorating the tree the expectations of Christmas have truly set in. A plain spruce would be too bare. That's why it's adorned with colourful decorations and candles. The green branches of the spruce generate a genuine feeling of summer amidst a sea of total darkness. Perhaps they also carry the faintest promise of a new spring.

A traditional Finnish Christmas Eve is hectic.

The morning comprises final preparations of food as well as wrapping up the very last presents. The spruce is brought in and decorated. Rice porridge and stewed mixed fruits are often eaten for lunch. After that, a family might very well have a sauna. The sauna whisk, frozen at midsummer, is dug out from the freezer. The heat of the sauna stove releases the fragrance of summer; birch permeates the bleakness. Next on the list is a quick visit to the cemetery to pay one's respect to deceased relatives. This touching ceremony includes the lighting of candles on the graves of loved ones. After this, it's back home for Christmas dinner. The dinner table is traditionally abundant. For starters there's slightly salted salmon, whitefish, herring, roe and salad of pickled herring and vegetables. This is followed by carrot, swede and potato casseroles and a huge roast ham with mustard sauce. For dessert there's coffee, Christmas pastries and fruit.

Christmas traditions vary somewhat from to region to region. There's always lively discussion concerning the correct way to celebrate a real Finnish Christmas. And after-dinner conversation invariably features an inquest into whether or not the ham was salty enough, etc.

Each generation creates their own traditions. Nowadays, people probably don't make as much fuss about Christmas as they used to. Christmas dishes have become lighter, reducing the need for people to go on crash diets immediately after the Christmas holidays. Many city dwellers have created their own international Christmas traditions. They might eat lobster, for example, washed down with champagne.

Children can hardly wait for the table to be cleared: an indication that the climax of the Finnish Christmas is about to take place. Father Christmas arrives at around eight in the evening. This old chap really is sprightly for his age; he can even visit several places at exactly the same time.

Korvatunturi

As everyone knows, Santa Claus lives in *Korvatunturi* in Finnish Lapland. All other claims are 'humbug'. It's from there that he starts his journey in a sledge pulled by reindeer. The sledge is stacked with presents for all the children in the world; well-behaved or otherwise. Father Christmas knocks on the door - usually with his staff - carrying the presents over his shoulder in a sack. Sometimes he's in such a hurry that he has to leave the sack on the doorstep or even toss it into the hallway, anonymously.

Eagerly unwrapping their presents, many Finnish children are delighted to discover they've been given winter sports equipment. After all, winter is well upon us.

Winter

Finland's snowy winter can be compared to an empty canvas - a 'tabula rasa' between an autumnal conception and the birth of a new spring. Finns like their winters white.

There's an old Finnish proverb that maintains that winter has no kin, meaning that every winter is different. Certainly, our winters have become even more unpredictable in recent years. Sometimes the whole country is frozen from top to bottom, sometimes it just rains for weeks on end. Pack ice, freezing winds and blizzards interspaced with temporary thawing can be a real test of endurance. But the Finnish winter can also be beautiful. In the depths of winter, when temperatures are well below zero, the skies can be spectacularly clear and starry. You can even go skiing by moonlight. The full moon illuminates the landscape, casting spooky shadows. Shooting stars maintain an all-night display, but we tend to keep a special lookout for winter's most amazing spectacle, the Aurora borealis.

Slushy days and sleety nights
Disappear with Northern Lights.

Bird watchers and wildlife enthusiasts look for tell-tale traces in the snow. Birds that weather the Finnish winter have to withstand extreme cold. The plumage of birds, such as the mallard, can stand temperatures as low as -70 to -80 degrees centigrade.

Snow also acts as a good insulator. Small rodents and many species of birds burrow themselves a winter refuge in the snow, a place to sleep. Nature's snowy nest stays safely above zero even when the air temperature reads otherwise.

The animals, of course, have stocked food for the winter. Likewise, the trees, bushes and hay make good use of their seeds for the winter vigil. People help the birds by providing them with food as well as places to feed. Bird tables are ubiquitous outside many houses, offering outdoor theatre for the audience within.

Conifers are unperturbed by freezing temperatures. Their needles freeze and defrost several times in the winter without suffering any harm. Nevertheless, the trees' picturesque but burdensome snowy mantels can cause considerable damage and even break their branches.

Snow and ice compel the scenery to undergo perpetual change. Even the most unpretentious little garden may take on a different appearance on a day-to-day basis, tailored by subtle changes in light and snow conditions.

Finland's winter is truly blue. The inescapable blueness of the shadows daubed on the snow is assured through the domination of blue light from an azure sky. Above the Arctic Circle people endure and enjoy the bluest and the longest of all Finnish moods; the Lapp winter. In Lapland, the sun only starts to peep over the horizon at the end of February, signalling the return of light and a hint of spring.

But sub-zero temperatures can't freeze biological urges. Romance raises its head as early as February. Foxes set about finding themselves a spouse. The female eagle is busy building her nest. Hares breed despite the cold; as do Finland's grey and ringed seals.

Finns love skiing in the woods. They carry sandwiches and coffee in their rucksacks. And, at the end of an invigorating, day-long skiing trip, nothing tastes better than thick pea soup followed by pancakes.

Some may wonder how an entire sea can freeze. Yet, that's invariably the fate that befalls the Baltic in wintertime. The ice can be up to a metre thick and easily takes the weight of a car. But Finns have learned to live with the conditions. Icebreakers crack open the shipping lanes so that life can go on as normal. And, thanks to a time-old tradition, most Finnish homes harbour more than a memory of summer: on a bitterly-cold day, when you're numbed to the marrow, you can always warm yourself up in the sauna.

Spring

The beginning of March sees the days getting appreciably longer. Light already starts to hold the upper hand. All kinds of creatures come out of hiding. People avidly sweep away the dust of winter, made only too apparent by the sunshine, and squint skywards.

Understandably, many Finns regard spring as their favourite season. New life unfolding is a joy to behold. The sun climbs higher and higher, bathing snowy rooftops in a relentless glow. The snow melts, only to freeze again in the cold of the night, leaving clusters of pointed icicles dangling under eaves.

The winter is noticeably devoid of smell. One of the first sensations of spring is the nondescript yet widespread smell of the ground thawing under the snow cover.

Finns have many rhymes and sayings about spring:

'Spring swings in a-swaying', meaning that the spring weather can swing abruptly from cold to warm, from calm to windy and from rain to sleet.

The order in which the birds return is also revealed in rhyme.

"One more moon," is skylark's tune.
"Two weeks, at least," chaffinch cheeps.
"Won't be long," chirps wagtail's song.
"Summer's here when swallows appear."

Perhaps that's the highlight of the spring in Finland; the return of the migratory birds. March heralds the start of the bird-watching season. The first southern storms help blow in the most spirited migrants. A sunny April morning in a tranquil forest can be a surprising setting for astonishingly loud bird song. Many people put bird boxes up in the trees. They're cleaned and repaired even as early as March in readiness for their inhabitants.

Everyone wants to enhance the arrival of spring in any way they can. Birch branches are brought inside and placed in vases for Eastertide. Within a few weeks they start developing bright green leaves, sometimes referred to as 'mouse's ears'. Already, they smell of summer. Bilberry twigs, if brought inside, effortlessly sprout leaves and are even known to flower.

The first wild flowers of spring strike a cheerful note. Yellow coltsfoot, peeking out along the roadside, is the first to catch the eye. Blue hepaticas and white wood anemones stand out between trunks of white birch. Alder is the first tree to bloom. It has already prepared its flowers the previous autumn. The warmth of the sun rapidly softens up the catkins. By mid-April, they're wide open.

The thawing of the soil frost heralds new life for the birch. If you press your ear against the trunk of a birch you will be able to hear the sap rising, in a headlong rush towards the top and branches. It's the perfect opportunity, if you have the patience, for milking the birch. Birch sap, a sweetish liquid, is packed with vitamins and favoured by athletes as an energizer.

Unlike many other kinds of breakups the Finnish one is a time for celebration. The ice squeaks, creaks and groans. Initially, waves or currents melt it from underneath. Then, slowly but surely, the ice starts to break away from the shore or bank, encouraged by a little wind. Even the thickest layer of ice has to give in eventually. The ice float drifts back and forth, ever-diminishing, till, like winter itself, it is no more.

Glossary

BERRIES AND FRUIT — MARJAT JA HEDELMÄT

arctic bramble	mesimarja
bilberry/blueberry	mustikka
blackcurrant	mustaviinimarja
cloudberry	lakka
cranberry	karpalo
gooseberry	karviainen
lingonberry /	
red whortleberry	puolukka
raspberry	vadelma
rowanberry	pihlajanmarja
sea buckthorn	tyrnimarja
strawberry	mansikka
apple	omena
lemon	sitruuna
orange	appelsiini
pear	päärynä
prune	kuivattu luumu
rhubarb	raparperi

BREAD — LEIPÄ

barley	ohra
buckwheat	tattari
corn	maissi
flour	jauho
plain/white flour	vehnäjauho
rye	ruis
unbleached flour	hiivaleipäjauho
(dried) yeast	(kuiva) hiiva

FISH — KALA

Baltic herring	silakka
burbot	made
cold-smoked	kylmäsavustettu
freshwater crayfish	rapu
perch	ahven
pike	hauki
pikeperch	kuha
rainbow trout	kirjolohi
roe	mäti
salmon	lohi
shrimp	katkarapu
slightly salted	graavattu
vendace	muikku
whitefish	siika

GAME — RIISTA

bear	karhu
elk, venison	hirvi
goose	hanhi
mallard	heinä/sinisorsa
pheasant	fasaani
reindeer	poro, peura
wild duck	sorsa
willow grouse	riekko

HERBS AND SPICES — YRTIT JA MAUSTEET

allspice	maustepippuri
basil	basilika
caraway	kumina
cardamom	kardemumma
chervil	kirveli
chives	ruohosipuli
cinnamon	kaneli
clove	neilikka
(flowering) dill	(kruunu) tilli
garlic	valkosipuli
ginger	inkivääri
juniper berry	katajanmarja
lemon balm	sitruunamelissa
nutmeg	muskottipähkinä
parsley	persilja
pepper	pippuri
rosemary	rosmariini
salt	suola
tarragon	rakuuna
thyme	timjami

MEAT — LIHA

bacon	pekoni
beef	nauta, härkä
fillet	filee
gammon/ham	kinkku
joint	paisti
lamb/mutton	lammas

MILK AND CHEESE — MAITO JA JUUSTO

Black label Emmenthal	mustaleima Emmenthal
blue cheese	aurajuusto
butter	voi
butter milk	kirnupiimä
(low-fat) curd cheese/	
quark	rahka
single cream	kahvikerma
sour cream	smetana
sour milk	piimä
whipping cream	kuohukerma
whole milk	kulutusmaito

MUSHROOMS — SIENET

champignon	herkkusieni
chanterelle	kanttarelli
cep	herkkutatti
(false) morel	korvasieni
milk cap	haaparousku/sieni
sheep Polyporus	lampaankääpä
trumpet chanterelle	suppilovahvero

VEGETABLES — VIHANNEKSET

asparagus	parsa
baking potato	uuniperuna
beetroot	punajuuri
bell pepper	paprika
broccoli	parsakaali
cabbage	kaali
carrot	porkkana
celeriac	juuriselleri
courgette/zucchini	kesäkurpitsa
cucumber	kurkku
fennel	fenkoli
horseradish	piparjuuri
kohlrabi	kyssäkaali
leek	purjo
lentil	linssi

lettuce	salaatti
onion	sipuli
parsnip	palsternakka
potato	peruna
radish	retiisi
spinach	pinaatti
swede/rutabaga	lanttu
tomato	tomaatti

MISCELLANEOUS | MUUTA

almond	manteli
baking powder	leivinjauhe
bicarbonate of soda	ruokasooda
breadcrumbs	korppujauhot
caper	kapris
gelatin	liivate
golden syrup	siirappi
honey	hunaja
jelly	hyytelö
malt	mallas
mayonnaise	majoneesi
mustard	sinappi
oil	öljy
pearl barley	ohrasuurimo
glutinous/	
porridge rice	puuroriisi
sap	mahla
soup	keitto
stock	liemi
(caster) sugar	(hieno) sokeri
vinegar	etikka

Bon Appétit! | Hyvää ruokahalua!

Conversion Tables

(rounded conversions)

GRAMS	OUNCES		MILLILITRES	IMPERIAL
25	1		150	1/4 pint
50	2		200	7 fl. oz.
75	3		250	9 fl. oz.
100	4		300	1/2 pint
150	5		425	3/4 pint
200	7		500	18 fl. oz.
250	9		600	1 pint
300	11		1000 ml (1 litre)	1 3/4 pints
400	14			
450	16 (1 lb)			
500	18			
1000 grams (1 kilo)	2.2 lb			

MILLILITRES	AMERICAN MEASURES		OVEN TEMPERATURES	
150	2/3 cup		150°C	300°F
200	1 cup		175°C	350°F
300	1 1/4 cups		200°C	400°F
425	2 cups		225°C	430°F
			250°C	480°F
			300°C	570°F

1 tablespoon (thsp) = one 15 ml spoon
1 teaspoon (tsp) = one 5 ml spoon
All spoon measures are level.

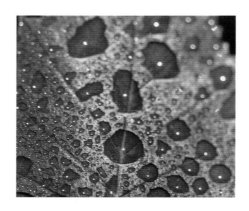

References:

Kotimaan luonto-opas, Wsoy (1994)
Kasvit: Teuvo Suominen
Sammalet, jäkälät ja sienet: Krister Karttunen
Linnut: Pertti Koskimies ja Juhani Lokki
Nisäkkäät: Petri Nummi
Kalat: Ulla Kokko
Kivet: Kalle Taipale
Talven sininen hetki Suomen luonnossa, Wsoy (1995)
Hulluna Sieniin, Wsoy (1995)
Vuokko Hosia, Sipa Westerholm
Kustaa Vilkunan vuotuinen ajantieto, Otava (1973)
Perinteinen Suomalainen keittiö, Vapk (1988)
Leena Heikkinen, Anita Patala

We would also like to thank the following magazines for their inspiring articles:
Suomen Luonto, Metsästys ja Kalastus, Erälehti and ET-lehti.